Manifesting with the Holy Spirit

by
C.B. Hedlun

My Crown of Grace Publishing

Spirit-led. Kingdom-focused.
Stories written with Heaven's ink.

C.B. Hedlun

Copyright © 2025 by C. B. Hedlun

All rights reserved. No part of this book may be reproduced, distributed, or transmitted in any form or by any means, including photocopying, recording, or other electronic or mechanical methods, without the prior written permission of the publisher, except in the case of brief quotations embodied in critical reviews and certain other noncommercial uses permitted by copyright law.

Scripture quotations are taken from the **World English Bible (WEB)**, which is in the public domain.

Published by **My Crown of Grace**

ISBN: 979-8-218-78333-4
Cover Design: CB Hedlun

For permissions, inquiries, or more information, please contact:

My Crown of Grace Publishing
Mycrownofgrace.com
[Oklahoma City, OK]

Printed in the United States of America

Manifesting with the Holy Spirit

Dedication

To God, the Author and Finisher of faith.

This book exists because of You. Every page, every word, every revelation was birthed through Your Spirit. In the moments I felt weak, You gave me strength. In the seasons I felt hidden, You reminded me I was being prepared. In the valleys I could not see through, You carried me until I could walk again.

Manifesting with the Holy Spirit is not my story alone—it is Yours. May it bring glory to Your name, healing to those who seek You, and light to those still walking in the shadows.
All I am, and all I create, I dedicate back to You.

Contact & Connect

For more resources, updates, and future books, visit:
  Website: mycrownofgrace.com
  Social Media: https://linktr.ee/cbhedlun
  Email inquiries: cheryl@mycrownofgrace.com

Author's Note

Simply put, I wrote this book because God told me to.

If I were to give a personal reason, it is this: there comes a moment in life when you realize you always knew, deep down, what your God-given purpose was. Long before enrolling in what I now call God's Ascension Bootcamp, I sensed that I was supposed to write a book before I died. Back then, I assumed it would be fiction.

In my early twenties, a religious studies professor once remarked that every society has a collective myth—except for America. That thought stuck with me. I wanted to create America's first collective myth, to build a world from scratch the way God created His. That dream led me to enroll in college at twenty-three. I thought I needed a lot of knowledge to write a fantasy adventure and make it sound believable—ironically, here I am, years later, writing a non-fiction book that by most standards sounds unbelievable. God does have a sense of humor.

Over the years I kept notes—quotes, storylines, fragments of imagination. But life always seemed to get in the way. I figured I'd finally write it after retirement. Then my daughter passed away. In my grief, I told God that the story would die with her—that it would be "the greatest story never told." I even threw away years of notes.

But God wasn't finished with me—or with the story. Ten years later, after walking through my own wilderness, I felt His presence press upon me, a fingertip covering my skull as He spoke into the deepest part of me: *"Stop looking for in others what only I can provide."* In that moment, something awakened.

From October 2024 onward, I began receiving what I can only describe as downloads—sudden bursts of knowing, visions, and instructions. My spiritual senses heightened, and I was slingshot into an accelerated program of awakening. Some days were exhilarating. Others, unbearably hard. But woven through it all was the unmistakable hand of the Holy Spirit, guiding me to write.

At first, I assumed God was bringing me back to the old fantasy adventure. But the further we adventured together, the clearer it became: the book I was created to write was not a myth of my own making, but a testimony of the journey He had taken me on. A map through wilderness and wonder. A record of ascension—not by self-effort, but by the Holy Spirit.

This is that book. It is my best effort to write down the path God asked me to walk so that others may follow. I don't claim to have gotten everything perfect, but I offer it as faithfully as I can.

If you are holding this book, I believe the Holy Spirit has brought it to you for a reason. My prayer is that within these pages, you will find what you need. And let me tell you—if you choose to walk this path—you are in for a wild ride.

—C.B. Hedlun

C.B.Hedlun

Table of Contents

CHAPTER ONE 9

CHAPTER TWO 23

CHAPTER THREE 49

CHAPTER FOUR 73

CHAPTER FIVE 92

CHAPTER SIX 109

CHAPTER SEVEN 131

CHAPTER EIGHT 147

CHAPTER NINE 166

CHAPTER TEN 183

CHAPTER ELEVEN 199

CHAPTER TWELVE 215

CHAPTER FOURTEEN 227

REFERENCES 249

Chapter One

Getting to Know the Holy Spirit

I didn't meet the Holy Spirit in a revival tent or a theology class. It was a random night, a YouTube rabbit hole that led me to a video from Gavin Dees. He prayed simply and said, "Invite the Holy Spirit to pour into you." That line exposed something in me: aside from the sign of the cross, I barely knew the Holy Spirit. My only frame of reference as of recent was a woman's near-death story—her husband had poisoned her, and in the paralysis the Holy Spirit comforted her. But who *is* He?

I'm not the only one who's foggy here. Surveys over the last decade—from Barna, Ligonier's State of Theology, and Pew—show that a surprising number of churchgoing Christians either think of the Holy Spirit as a symbol of God's power or they aren't sure how to describe Him at all. No wonder we lurch between two ditches: silence on one side (He's rarely mentioned) and sensationalism on the other (He's reduced to caricature—strange stunts and spiritual theatrics). If that's the menu, the everyday believer is left unsure what's real.

Here's why that matters: you can't teach about Someone you don't actually know. Without the Holy Spirit's living presence and gifts, churches quietly train people to expect less from God than what He's promised. Without intimacy, theology stays abstract. However, the Holy Spirit is not an "it," not mist or mood. He is God Himself—personal, present, holy.

Jesus' words are straightforward: "I will ask the Father, and he will give you another Counselor, that he may be with you forever—the Spirit of truth" (John 14:16-17). He indwells (John 14:17), teaches and guides (John 16:13), convicts (John 16:8), empowers (Acts 1:8), and even prays through us when we don't have words (Romans 8:26-27). That's not a force; that's a Person.

If you've been burned by hype or bored by silence, this book is my hand on your shoulder saying: there's a third way. Not performance. Not avoidance. *Presence.* Manifesting with the Holy Spirit isn't about staging moments; it's about learning to walk with the One Jesus promised would live inside you—therefore, what "abundance" means gets redefined: not just money, but healing, purpose, peace, courage, daily bread. If you've ever wondered whether there's more to the Christian life, there is. He has a name.

What "Manifesting" Means

Human beings have always sensed that reality contains more than what the eye can see. Today, many people try to access that "more" through ideas circulating in popular spirituality. In the secular world, "manifesting" usually means something like this: set a clear intention, visualize it vividly, rehearse new beliefs until they feel true, and—so the promise goes—the universe will rearrange itself around you.

I sampled that shelf. Dr. Joe Dispenza's meditations on the "quantum field." Neville Goddard's law of assumption and revision. Alan Watts' poetic philosophy. Abraham Hicks' language about the vortex. The list goes on. Some of it helped me focus, and some of it quieted anxiety for a while. But the more I practiced, the more a quiet question kept tugging at my sleeve: *Who is the source here—me, or God?*

That question matters because in many Christian circles the word *manifesting* immediately raises suspicion. It sounds too close to witchcraft or New Age spirituality. And in some forms, that concern is justified. Secular manifesting often treats the human mind as the creative force shaping reality.

But the enemy does not create new things. He distorts what God has already made. If a distortion exists, that means an original design exists too.

Scripture shows this pattern again and again. What someone intends for harm, God can intend for good (Genesis 50:20). Fear may appear in the world, but God does not give us a spirit of fear (2 Timothy 1:7). Wherever we see something twisted, we are often looking at a truth that has been bent out of shape.

So the answer is not panic. It is discernment.

When something appears in culture, the question is not simply, "Everyone is doing it—should I join them?" Nor is it, "Reject it immediately without looking." The better question is this: *What part of this reflects God's design, and what part is the distortion?*

That is where the Holy Spirit becomes essential. Secular manifesting aims to attract outcomes. Spirit-led manifesting aims to agree with God.

Jesus does not say, "Apart from the right technique you can do nothing." He says, "Apart from me you can do nothing" (John 15:5). The goal stops being control and becomes communion. Abundance begins to look different too—not simply acquiring things, but receiving substance: healing in places therapy could not reach, purpose that outlasts changing moods, peace that does not hinge on circumstances, courage for the day in front of you, and daily bread even when the numbers say it should not be enough (Romans 14:17; 2 Corinthians 9:8).

Looking back, I can see the difference in the fruit. The secular tools helped me organize emotions and sharpen focus, but the Holy Spirit began transforming me (2 Corinthians 3:18). One manages mental state; the Other remakes the heart. One says, "Generate a frequency." The Other says, "Abide in me, and I will supply the life" (John 15:4–5). One tries to bend reality from the outside; the Other writes God's will on the inside and then walks you into it (Romans 12:2).

This shift also changed the way I interpreted some of my early experiences. I would receive sudden promptings, images, or phrases that seemed to arrive with unusual weight. The secular framework might describe this as intuition training. The Kingdom uses a different picture: sheep learning to recognize the voice of their Shepherd (John 10:27).

Instead of trying to command the universe, I learned to respond to the Holy Spirit—ask, listen, test, obey. Sometimes He said "wait." Sometimes He said "no." And sometimes, in the middle of my weakness, He met me with strength I did not have (2 Corinthians 12:9).

So here's my working definition now: Manifesting with the Holy Spirit is agreement with God's will through intimacy with God's Spirit. It isn't passivity; it's partnership. I bring a yielded heart, honest prayers in Jesus' name, and small obedient steps. He brings presence, guidance, conviction, comfort, timing, and power (John 16:13; Romans 8:26–27). The result isn't just that things change; it's that I change—and then the right things change with me.

If you've tried the vision boards and mantras and still feel hollow, you're not broken. You may just need a new Teacher. The world teaches you to self-program. Jesus sends the Counselor to indwell (John 14:16–17). One is you carrying your future; the other is God carrying you into His.

The Voice That Changed Everything

It was August 2024. I had just finished my master's in public administration, with an emphasis in health management, and was working as a Medicare biller for three long-term care facilities. I had chosen this path in 2022, when I knew I would one day become the legal guardian of my sister's three children after her passing. The years in between were a blur of surviving grief, adjusting careers, and planning for a future that always seemed to demand another backup plan.

At work, the monotony of billing reports left me searching for something to keep my mind alive. That's how I stumbled across social media lectures on quantum physics with Dr. Dispenza and Dr. Bruce Lipton. I was fascinated by their claims that thought could reshape biology, that belief could alter the subconscious, that energy and matter were two sides of the same reality. I shared their videos online, hoping someone else would be intrigued. But no one was watching with me.

By October, the weight of silence was heavy. Another failed round of online dating. More résumés ignored. More nights of wondering if I was invisible to the world. Then a turning point arrived. Like many nights, my dog woke me up between 3–5 a.m. I had seen videos claiming this hour was when the veil between worlds was thin. Curious but mostly desperate, I decided to try manifesting.

I sat on my bed, closed my eyes, and began imagining a relationship—picturing reconciling with someone from my past. That's when God broke in.

"Really? That's what you're going with?"

Maybe you've wondered what it would be like to hear God's voice yourself—whether it would sound like your thoughts, or something completely different. For me, the sound of His voice was unlike anything I had ever heard. It wasn't the usual chatter of my own thoughts, nor the voice of my imagination. It was my own inner voice, yes—but magnified, resonant, thundering with a weight I couldn't deny. It carried clarity and power so strong that I knew instantly: this was not me.

That night, I had stumbled into what Christian mystics used to write about with poetic language—what we now might call clairaudience, clear-hearing through the veil between heaven and earth. For centuries, the saints described it as the "small voice of God," or a "heavenly sound," but modern readers often miss that they were talking about the same sixth-sense capabilities believers still carry today. In modern spirituality these experiences are often labeled clairaudience or clairvoyance. Scripture describes them more simply: learning to recognize the voice of the Shepherd (John 10:27) and perceiving the guidance of the Holy Spirit.

The truth is, these gifts were never meant to be rare or reserved for a chosen few. When the Holy Spirit was poured out, He came for all flesh (Acts 2:17). Every believer carries within them spiritual senses—ways to see, hear, and perceive God. But today, many Christians are afraid of words like "clairaudience" or "clairvoyance." They hear those terms and think of psychics, witches, or something forbidden. And so, instead of recognizing these sensitivities as holy, people are shamed for them. Some get pushed out of the Church entirely. Others bury their gifts, believing they are a curse. Or like me, they are confused not knowing what was happening. That's where much of church hurt comes from—leaders trying to teach about Someone they have never truly met themselves.

And when gifts are silenced or suppressed, people often turn to lesser spirits for affirmation. They lower their sense of worth, settling for communion with what feels accessible "on their level," rather than lifting their gifts back to the Holy Spirit—the only One who can sanctify and direct them.

But imagine if we saw it differently. Imagine if every whisper, vision, or holy nudge was recognized for what it truly is: an invitation into intimacy with God. The shame and guilt would fall away. No one would feel exiled for hearing His voice. Instead, the Church could become a place where the sensitive are taught, guided, and encouraged to lean in deeper. Because these aren't curses—they're callings.

That night, I didn't yet understand any of this. All I knew was that God had spoken, and I was terrified. I yanked the covers over my head and pretended to be asleep. But His voice lingered, heavy and undeniable. And I realized—I just might have gotten myself into trouble.

Trouble, as it turns out, was the beginning of everything. Professor of Literature, mythologist, writer, and lecturer Joseph Campbell refers to it in his Monomyth theory as the hero's call to adventure—that moment when the ordinary world collides with the extraordinary, when you are invited into transformation. God wasn't mocking me when He asked, "Really? That's what you're going with?" He was redirecting me. Manifestation wasn't about twisting reality to match my desires. It was about surrendering my imagination to His.

The more I reflected, the clearer it became. Science had fascinated me— Dr. Lipton showing that atoms are mostly space, whirling like tiny vortexes, reminding me of how the Holy Spirit moves in, through, and around all things. Dr. Dispenza teaching how thought rewires the brain and body. But the more I listened, the more impossible it seemed to manifest without the Holy Spirit. Science could explain patterns, but it couldn't breathe life into them. Without Him, it all fell flat.

Hitting the Glass Ceiling

I began to notice I wasn't the only one struggling with secular manifestation. Friends, coworkers, even strangers online were saying the same thing: *"Manifesting doesn't work."*

Maybe you've tried it before—setting intentions, making vision boards, repeating affirmations—only to end up discouraged when nothing seemed to happen. What I discovered was that the missing piece wasn't my technique. It was *who* I was manifesting with.

Did the playlists, affirmations, and vision boards help me realize what I wanted? Sure. But they couldn't heal the places that were broken. The Holy Spirit could. He began shattering chains, pruning away what was weighing me down, and sanctifying my imagination so it served love instead of lack.

The Holy Spirit doesn't simply give us what we want. He reshapes what we want so that it aligns with God's will, allowing the fruit to last. Over time He taught me that manifestation is not about self-glory—it is about Kingdom glory. The gifts God gives are never meant to terminate in us; they are meant to flow outward.

But that way of living runs against the cultural current of the modern West, particularly in America, where the American Dream often reigns supreme. We are taught to chase the flame—passion, excitement, self-expression, self-fulfillment. Personal happiness becomes the highest goal. Follow your heart. Build your brand. Live your truth.

That phrase—*live your truth*—sounds empowering, but it quietly assumes something profound: that truth originates within us. Even in the Church, we sometimes slip into this mindset, picking and choosing the parts of faith we prefer while setting aside the ones that challenge us. In that sense, the ancient story of the forbidden fruit still echoes in our culture. Humanity's first temptation was not simply disobedience—it was the desire to define good and evil for ourselves.

Love, however—the kind God models—is what remains after the spark fades. It stays when the excitement dies down. It chooses what is best for another person—even when that choice costs something. True love does not begin with the question, *What do I want?* It begins with the question, *What will help them flourish?*

For most of human history, life was centered on the "we"—the clan, the village, the parish, the guild. People shared labor, shared meals, and shared burdens. Life was understood as something carried together.

In the modern West, however, rugged individualism hardened into something like a cultural catechism. Identity became something we construct and promote. Worth became something we measure by productivity. Even our relationships became curated through screens. We live stacked above strangers in apartment towers—surrounded by people, yet often unknown to them.

Sociologist Robert Putnam famously described this unraveling as "bowling alone," pointing to the decline of civic participation and neighborly trust. Philosopher Charles Taylor traced the same shift to what he calls a "secular age," one that elevates the self-defining individual as the center of meaning.

The result is a strange paradox: a society more connected than ever technologically, yet filled with people who feel increasingly isolated. Disembodied souls wander through crowded cities—lonelier, more anxious, and less convinced that their flourishing is tied to anyone else's.

Community used to be the operating system. Now the self is. When life becomes entirely about "me," we forget how to receive and how to give. We forget that our lives were meant to be intertwined. This self-centered vision of life is not simply unfortunate—it is sinful. It pulls us away from the very design God intended for human beings.

The life of the Spirit moves in the opposite direction. The Holy Spirit continually draws us back into humility, cooperation, and love that overflows for the sake of others.

Because the Kingdom of God was never meant to be built around the self. It was always meant to be built around love.

Even biology hints at this: Dr. Lipton notes in *The Wisdom of Your Cells* that "survival of the fittest" doesn't actually guarantee survival—cooperation does. From cells forming tissues to organisms thriving in ecosystems, harmony and coordinated support are the natural strategy for life. In the same way, we manifest with the Holy Spirit not to hoard blessings, but to pour them out—so God's glory is revealed and others are drawn closer.

That's what humans miss when they covet power—to keep it, to claim it, to make it theirs. But even God Himself doesn't do that. His power is always shared, always given, always moving outward. And that is why manifesting with the Holy Spirit will never be about possession or control. It will always be about testimony, love, and the glory of God.

Even storytellers have glimpsed this truth. Hans Christian Andersen once said, "Life itself is the most wonderful fairy tale." For him, imagination and belief weren't fantasy; they were the lens through which we glimpse God's larger story. Goddard, too, emphasized the power of imagination to shape reality. And while he was right about its power, he missed the most important part: imagination must be surrendered to the Holy Spirit. Without Him, imagination caves inward. With Him, imagination becomes a doorway for God's Kingdom to unfold in us.

It struck me one day that the pattern of creation itself is the pattern we're invited to walk in. God imagined the heavens and the earth, believed in us, and then spoke creation into being: "Let there be light" (Genesis 1:3). That rhythm—imagination, faith, spoken word—still pulses through everything. When I manifest with the Holy Spirit, I'm not playing at being God, I'm leaning into His design. I bring Him my imagination, let Him align it with faith, and then release it through words and actions. And always, it circles back to His glory, not mine. Like Paul wrote, "I planted, Apollos watered, but God gave the increase" (1 Corinthians

3:6). My part is to testify, to witness, to water. The Holy Spirit is the One who makes things grow.

Beautiful in theory, yes—but it's also muscle memory you build. Writing this book has forced me to practice what I'm preaching: to write for formation, not applause; to prefer growth over being "the next fresh perspective." (Full disclosure: if someone calls me brilliant, I won't faint from offense.) Still, most of the big connections didn't come from my cleverness; they arrived like downloads—what some call claircognizance and what I, as a Christian, recognize as breakthrough insight from the Holy Spirit. My work has been to stay humble, keep my heart uncluttered, and show up on the page. His work has been to breathe on the seed, turn sparks into sentences, and keep me honest when ego tries to grab the pen.

I've learned the Holy Spirit doesn't let me skip the part where faith and trust get tested either. Faith has felt less like a concept and more like currency I had to spend, sometimes when my pockets felt empty. Jesus once promised, "Whoever believes in me, the works that I do, he will do also; and he will do greater works than these" (John 14:12). I used to think that sounded impossible. Now I know it means faith is believing before I see, moving before I feel ready, and acting like God has already spoken. Emanuel Swedenborg was right—faith without love is hollow, like a bubble that bursts the second you touch it. Real faith is alive when it's joined with love and lived in trust of Christ Himself.

And then there's trust. Trust, as I have come to learn, is what steadies me when prayers hang in the air unanswered, when seasons stretch on longer than I think I can bear, when outcomes don't look like what I expected. Proverbs has whispered to me more times than I can count: "Trust in Yahweh with all your heart, and don't lean on your own understanding" (Proverbs 3:5-6). It's one thing to quote it; it's another to live it when the ground feels like it's falling out from under your feet.

T.S. Eliot once wrote in *Four Quartets:* "I said to my soul, be still, and wait... the faith and the love and the hope are all in the waiting." I've carried those words like a prayer. Trust isn't throwing up my hands and giving up. It's sitting still in the emotion when I want to run, waiting when I want to fix, and letting the Holy Spirit set the pace when I'd rather sprint.

What I've found is that when imagination, faith, and trust finally come together under the Holy Spirit's leading, it becomes the living proof that God is real, that His Spirit is here, and that my life—scarred, messy, and still being healed—can shine as evidence of His presence. People may doubt doctrine or dismiss theology, but they cannot deny a life transformed. And that, more than anything, is the wonder of manifesting with the Holy Spirit.

Chapter Two

Early Lessons in Walking with the Holy Spirit

Joseph Campbell, the mythologist who studied the stories of cultures across the world, noticed something remarkable: many of humanity's greatest stories follow the same pattern. An ordinary person receives a call to adventure. At first the call is confusing, even unsettling. The hero rarely understands what it means. Yet once the journey begins, mentors appear, trials emerge, and tools are given along the way—each one preparing the traveler for the road ahead.

Campbell called this pattern the monomyth, or the Hero's Journey. Long before scholars put language to it, Scripture had already been telling the same story.

Abraham heard a call to leave the familiar and walk toward a promise he could not yet see. Moses encountered God in the wilderness before being sent back to confront Pharaoh. David was anointed king long before he ever sat on the throne. Even Mary received a promise she could not possibly explain before she carried it quietly in her heart.

God's pattern has always been the same: the call comes first, and the training follows.

The night the Holy Spirit interrupted my attempt at secular manifestation, I did not realize that I had stepped onto a similar road. At the time it felt less like an epic adventure and more like stumbling into a conversation I was completely unprepared to have. I knew something had shifted, but I had no map for what came next.

And that is where many people find themselves when they first begin manifesting with the Holy Spirit.

The initial encounter can feel electrifying. Suddenly prayers feel alive. Synchronicities begin appearing. Thoughts and impressions carry unusual weight. It feels as if a hidden dimension of life has opened. But the excitement of the call often comes before the wisdom to interpret what is happening.

In other words, the adventure has begun—but the traveler has not yet been trained.

That early stage can be fragile. It is easy to speak too quickly about things we do not yet understand. It is easy to misinterpret signs and symbols through the lens of the secular ideas we already know. It is easy to assume that personal transformation means the whole world is about to end. And it is easy to underestimate the testing that follows when God begins forming someone for a purpose in His Kingdom.

Scripture shows that God rarely sends His people onto the road without preparation. Just as a seasoned guide equips travelers before they enter unfamiliar terrain, the Holy Spirit provides wisdom for those learning to walk this narrow path. These lessons are not meant to discourage the journey. They are meant to protect it. Think of them as tools for the road ahead.

Some tools guard the seed of what God has begun. Others help you interpret the changes happening in your life. Some prepare you for the quiet tests that shape character. And some help you understand why opposition often appears the moment a new calling begins to take root.

Trailblazers do not start their journeys fully formed. They begin as ordinary people who are willing to listen, learn, and keep walking even when the path feels uncertain. Over time, the road they travel becomes a map for others who will follow behind them.

This chapter explores several of the early lessons the Holy Spirit often teaches when someone first begins manifesting with Him. They are not rules so much as guideposts—wisdom that helps protect what God is growing before it is ready to stand in the open.

When God plants a promise in your life, the goal is not simply that you reach the destination. The goal is that you become the kind of person who can guide others along the way. Like every hero's journey, the road begins with learning how to carry the call wisely.

Learning the Language of Biblical Symbols

Many people who come to faith from the secular world already understand the idea of symbols and synchronicities. Psychology talks about archetypes and dream imagery. Popular spirituality talks about signs, repeating numbers, and the universe sending messages. So when someone first begins noticing patterns or symbols appearing in their life, the instinct is to interpret them using those familiar frameworks. The challenge is that the Holy Spirit tends to speak through a different symbolic language.

Instead of angel numbers, the language of the Holy Spirit is usually rooted in Scripture. The symbols, metaphors, and patterns come from the biblical story itself. Tools like Strong's Concordance, the Gematria Calculator, or even studying Hebrew word meanings can become far more helpful than the methods often promoted in modern spirituality. The difference is subtle but important. Instead of inventing meaning, the goal is to anchor interpretation in the symbolic world that the Bible already uses.

I had to learn that lesson the hard way.

During the same season when my life was shifting under the surface, symbols began appearing everywhere, almost like breadcrumbs scattered along a path. Eagles seemed to show up constantly—on commercials, gas-station packaging, even a small decal tucked into a mountain wall mural I had ordered for my office. Wolves appeared in unexpected places. Horses. Lighthouses. The images felt strangely persistent, as if something was trying to catch my attention.

Symbols themselves were not new to me. Because of my Irish roots, I had grown up around folklore and symbolic storytelling. Later, after my child passed away, I experienced a number of moments that felt like signs encouraging me to keep going. Those experiences had already opened my mind to the idea that life sometimes communicates through symbols and patterns.

The problem was not recognizing the symbols. The problem was knowing how to interpret them.

The only tools I had at the time came from the secular world—dream dictionaries, folklore interpretations, and psychological symbolism. Those frameworks can be helpful in their own way, but they are not designed to interpret the language of Scripture. When the Holy Spirit began speaking through biblical imagery, I was trying to translate it using the wrong dictionary.

Then came the symbols that felt far more personal and uncomfortable: pregnancy and babies.

Around November I sensed the Holy Spirit telling me to stop searching for a job and trust that one would come to me. That instruction was not as difficult to obey as it might sound. At the time, every hiring algorithm seemed determined to chew up my résumé and spit it out before a human being ever saw it. So I waited. Eventually a recruiter found me through LinkedIn, scheduled an interview, coached me through the process, and within a few weeks I had a new position. It was not a dramatic promotion—more of a sideways step—but I sensed the Holy Spirit nudging me to accept it.

The woman assigned to train me: pregnant.

Those images carried a weight that went far beyond symbolism for me. My only child had died at fourteen, a loss that shattered my world in ways I did not know how to articulate at the time. Not long afterward I had to undergo a hysterectomy. The part of my body that had carried my daughter—the last physical connection to bringing her into the world—was gone. Along with it went any possibility of having another child.

The year after she died, it seemed as if everyone around me was announcing pregnancies. Friends, acquaintances, coworkers—everywhere I looked, people were celebrating new life while I was still trying to understand how mine had ended. Whether anyone meant it this way or not, the comparisons felt brutal. In the quiet places of my mind I began forming a painful conclusion: maybe God had taken my child because I had done something wrong, and maybe He was giving other people new children because they had done something right.

That kind of thinking isolates you quickly. In our culture, when tragedy happens people instinctively look for someone to blame. Job knew it—he lost wealth, health, and children, then watched friends moralize his pain. That reflex to blame the suffering isn't just ancient; it's human. Psychologists call it the "just-world" phenomenon—our mind's urge to assume people get what they deserve—so we can feel safe, even when we're watching someone else bleed (Lerner, 1980). We've seen it in headlines and classrooms: the way crowds go quiet and look away (the bystander effect first mapped after the Kitty Genovese case), the way ordinary people can be talked into doing what they swore they'd never do (Milgram, 1963), the way a role or a label can turn a heart hard in a hurry (the Stanford prison study). Left to ourselves, we explain away pain or participate in it. Without the Holy Spirit, we're more likely to protect our comfort than comfort the broken.

Parents who lose children to suicide often carry the heaviest version of that burden. Sometimes the accusations are spoken out loud. Other times they remain unspoken but painfully implied. Here's the darker confession: when the world blamed me, I joined them. After my daughter died, the voice in my head learned all their lines. Shame became scripture. And somewhere along the way I made a private agreement: if I heal, I'm a bad mother. If the PTSD eases, if the panic softens, if the flashbacks stop—what does that say about my love? I told myself good mothers hurt forever. Carrying my pain felt like proof that I still deserved the title.

That's the cruelest trick in the war of the mind. The enemy can't create life, so he forges contracts—lies that sound like virtue: your grief equals your love; your fear equals your wisdom; your self-accusation equals your humility. He keeps you "faithful" to your wound by convincing you that healing is betrayal. Meanwhile, he bleeds your hope dry.

In that confusion I quietly stepped away from the parts of life that reminded me of what I had lost. Babies and pregnancy became one of those things.

So when those same symbols began appearing again nearly a decade later—pregnancy, babies, images of new life—I dismissed them almost immediately. Whatever they meant, they could not possibly apply to me. That chapter of my life had closed permanently.

At least, that was what I believed at the time.

Around the same time another image began appearing in my mind's eye throughout the day, and this one was far more awkward. I kept seeing flashes of male anatomy—specifically testicles. The experience was mortifying. I had just repented and was trying to live a cleaner life with the Holy Spirit. The last thing I expected was for explicit imagery to start appearing randomly in my thoughts. I kept wondering why this image would not go away.

It took months before the meaning became clear.

The "key" came when I was drawn back to Mary's story in Scripture. In the language of the Bible, pregnancy is often used as a metaphor for promises conceived. The Bible frequently speaks about labor pains, birthing, and new life as images of spiritual transformation. The symbolism is woven throughout Scripture.

Then the other piece finally made sense. Testicles symbolize seed.

In Luke 8:11 Jesus explains one of His own parables by saying, "The seed is the word of God." Peter later writes that believers are "born again… through the living and enduring word of God," describing that rebirth as coming through an incorruptible seed (1 Peter 1:23). What had felt embarrassing and confusing at first turned out to be a blunt symbolic reminder: God had planted something, and I was being asked to carry it.

Apparently, there is a learning curve to Holy Spirit-speak.

Mary's Pattern: Conceive Quietly, Carry Faithfully

When something extraordinary begins unfolding in your life, the first instinct is usually to tell someone. Not only because it amazes you, but because you want confirmation that what you're sensing is real. You want someone else to see what you're seeing. Yet the earliest stages of God's promises are often the most delicate. They are still forming, still growing, still hidden beneath the surface. Share them too quickly with people who cannot see what God is doing, and the seed may be trampled before it takes root. Scripture shows us a different pattern: before a promise becomes public testimony, it is often carried quietly in the heart.

Mary's story doesn't begin with proof; it begins with a word. A messenger speaks what she cannot possibly verify yet, and she says yes (Luke 1:26–38). Then she does something most of us struggle to do in an age of instant announcements—she keeps it close. "Mary kept all these sayings, pondering them in her heart" (Luke 2:19). Early on, promises are fragile. They need warmth, quiet, and covering. Many won't "get it" because they weren't given your word. Protect the seed—choose quiet obedience over noisy proof.

After the night God called me out, my life shifted into what I can only describe as a first trimester of the spirit. Something new had begun growing inside my life, but it was still invisible—fragile, forming beneath the surface.

As I began walking with Him more intentionally, the changes were subtle at first. I didn't immediately feel like a different person. In fact, what struck me most was not how I had changed, but how the people around me seemed to respond differently.

Conversations that once felt natural suddenly felt strained. Words that used to land easily now seemed to drift past people like the muffled voices in a Charlie Brown cartoon—*wah wah wah*. Friends and family I had known for years began reacting to things I said with confusion, irritation, or quiet dismissal. It was as if we were speaking the same language but no longer understanding each other.

At the time, I didn't know what to make of it. I wasn't trying to provoke anyone. I was simply sharing what I was witnessing—what the Holy Spirit was beginning to show me. But for some reason, it seemed to leave a bad taste in people's mouths.

Later I began to understand what might have been happening. Dr. Lipton often describes how our internal beliefs and emotional patterns shape the signals our bodies operate under, almost like tuning a radio frequency. As the Holy Spirit began reshaping my thoughts and desires, something in my inner signal was shifting.

When a frequency changes, the stations that once came in clearly start to sound like static. Connections that once felt magnetic can suddenly feel misaligned. It wasn't that I had consciously decided to distance myself from people. It was simply that the wavelength we had once shared no longer carried the same signal.

Hell wants to destroy every seed heaven plants. That's why premature announcements draw fire. God didn't give your vision to everyone else—so they can't see what you see, and most people prefer comfort over change. When your life starts to shift, they'll try to put you back where you "fit" so the world makes sense again. The enemy uses that reflex. He loves group comfort because it keeps you small.

When Your World Feels Like It's Ending

When old patterns begin breaking, when beliefs shift, when relationships change, and when your internal compass starts pointing in a different direction, the ground beneath your feet can feel unstable. The structures that once made life predictable begin to move. From the inside, that upheaval can feel dramatic, almost apocalyptic. My first interpretation of that upheaval was exactly that: the world must be ending. After all, why else would God suddenly start speaking to me?

Naturally, I assumed I had been recruited as some kind of emergency broadcast system for humanity. Clearly my job was to warn everyone to repent immediately before whatever cosmic event was about to happen. There was just one problem. The Holy Spirit kept hinting that I should keep quiet. At the time that didn't make sense to me. God wants people saved. God wants truth shared. Surely the loving thing to do was warn everyone about what I thought was coming. I also believed I had enough credibility for people to take my warning seriously. Eventually, after ignoring those quiet nudges long enough, it felt as though God simply allowed me to follow my own assumption.

So I told people. Go on, take a wild guess how well that went over. If I remember correctly, I was told to stop scaring everyone and return to my psychiatrist and therapist to get my head straight.

The experience was humbling, but it revealed something important. What is actually ending are the internal structures that once shaped your life: old attachments, old thought patterns, old coping mechanisms, and old identities. Chains begin breaking. Roots begin getting pulled up. Appetites begin changing. From the inside, that kind of internal demolition can feel dramatic, but what is really happening is the quiet dismantling of a life that can no longer hold what God is building.

When the global catastrophe I had predicted stubbornly refused to arrive, my mind swung to the opposite conclusion. Maybe the world was not ending. Maybe I was. One afternoon, while driving home through tornado weather, I called my mom to give her a running list of revelations I had not yet written down, just in case I was about to be raptured or carried off by a tornado before I could finish recording them. Looking back now, I can laugh at how intense those early interpretations were, but in the moment they felt very real. What the Holy Spirit was actually saying was far simpler and far wiser: your old world is ending, and that is a necessary part of transformation.

This is where discernment becomes essential. In the early stages of walking with God, it is easy to assume that every revelation should immediately be shared with everyone. But the Holy Spirit rarely trains people for public influence by throwing them onto a stage overnight. More often He trains them quietly. Scripture shows this pattern repeatedly.

Consider Elijah. When he first appears in the biblical story, he bursts onto the scene with bold authority, declaring a drought over Israel in the name of the Lord. Soon afterward he confronts hundreds of prophets of Baal on Mount Carmel and calls down fire from heaven. It is one of the most dramatic demonstrations of God's power in the entire Bible. Yet immediately afterward Elijah collapses emotionally and runs for his life from Queen Jezebel. Exhausted and overwhelmed, he flees into the wilderness and tells God he would rather die than continue.

God's response is revealing. Instead of sending Elijah back into another public confrontation, God begins by caring for his exhaustion. Elijah is fed, allowed to rest, and led into isolation on a mountain. When God finally speaks to him, it is not through the wind, the earthquake, or the fire, but through a gentle whisper. Before Elijah could carry God's voice publicly, he had to learn to hear God's voice quietly.

The pattern has not changed. When God prepares someone to speak, He shapes the message through humility, wisdom, and timing. He trains discernment. He forms character. He strips away pride and replaces it with dependence. One of the uncomfortable lessons I eventually learned was that the less you tell, the more credibility you keep. This is not secrecy born from fear but privacy born from stewardship. God often grows a calling in private before revealing it publicly. There is a season where you learn to hear His voice, interpret what He is showing you, and test what you think you understand. Later He may open doors for you to share those insights, but even then the training usually begins in small places—conversations with trusted friends, moments with family, and quiet acts of obedience that no audience ever sees.

Over time I learned a principle that has served me well: announce later, obey first. When God truly prepares someone to speak, He ensures the message is shaped by humility, wisdom, and timing. And voices shaped that way rarely begin by shouting that the world is ending.

Pop Quizzes in Real Time

If you need to talk to someone about what God is doing in your life, talk to Him first. Talk to Him in the secret place and let everyone else witness the fruit in due time. And yes, I mean talk to Him the way you would speak to someone close to you. I have passed more pop quizzes than I can count simply by telling God what happened that day, what bothered me, how it made me feel, and what I thought about it. I have even told Him when I felt like He misunderstood what I meant.

Those small moments turned out to be far more important than I realized at the time. They were like pop quizzes of the heart. Not tests of knowledge, but tests of posture. God already knows what is inside us, but we often do not see it until life presses on it. In those moments He seems to be asking quiet questions: *Will you bring this to Me first? Will you trust Me here?*

Sometimes the quiz reveals we are not ready yet. Sometimes it confirms that we are. And sometimes it simply becomes a marker in the journey—a moment you can look back on later when doubt creeps in and remember, *No, God really did lead me here.*

Walking with the Holy Spirit often feels like walking in partial light. You rarely see the whole road ahead. Most of the time you only see the next step, and that can be unsettling if you are the kind of person who prefers maps.

What begins in silence is almost always tested in the noise of real life. Eventually the moment comes when faith has to stand in the middle of circumstances that make God's word look unlikely. That moment came for me sooner than I expected.

The phone rings like an air-raid siren. An unknown number. Then another. Voicemail starts piling up—polite threats that do not feel polite. Rent is due. You are doing the thing God asked you to do...and it looks like He is cutting it close.

This is where the first arrow almost always lands: *"Did God really say...?"* (Genesis 3:1).

It rarely arrives as a dramatic debate. It is usually a whisper that slides under the door and settles in your chest. *Did I hear wrong? Did I make this up? Am I holding God to a promise He never actually gave?*

People often say, "God will provide for what He has called you to do." But when you are in the middle of the test, the question becomes more uncomfortable: *What if He doesn't?*

You replay everything in your mind. *Was that really His word, or something I borrowed from people who talk about His word? Did I embellish it somewhere along the way?* The clock keeps ticking. The enemy seems to have already breached the gates. You feel outnumbered. God told you to stand here until He returns—but it is starting to look like He is taking His time getting back.

Then another phrase people say lands like a stone in your chest: "The enemy can only attack as God allows."

Do you know how terrifying that thought can be when you are the one under attack? Who do you file a complaint with when the person who allowed it is God?

At one point I remember telling God what Jesus had done to me—fully aware that I was telling Jesus what Jesus had done to me. Petty, maybe. Honest, absolutely. Because when you are in that place, the question becomes unavoidable: *If God is against you, what then?*

Why Does God Allow the Attack?

Looking back, I can also see another spiritual principle that I did not understand at the time. It is a pattern that appears in the story of Balaam.

In the book of Numbers, a king named Balak hires the prophet Balaam to curse Israel. Balaam tries repeatedly, but every time he opens his mouth, blessing comes out instead of a curse. The reason is simple: God had already blessed His people, and Balaam could not reverse what God had spoken.

But the story does not end there.

Later we learn that Balaam discovered another strategy. If Israel could not be cursed from the outside, they could be tempted from the inside. By drawing them into idolatry and compromise, Balaam showed Balak how to lure God's people into stepping outside the protection of their covenant with God. Once they responded to that temptation, the door opened for destruction to enter their camp.

The lesson is sobering.

The enemy cannot easily destroy what God protects. So instead of attacking directly, he often works through temptation. If he can draw someone away from God's wisdom and into compromise, the protection that once surrounded them becomes harder to recognize.

For a long time I believed that tragedy meant God was punishing me. But as I began studying Scripture more deeply, I realized something different was happening. My life had not been aligned with God's wisdom in many areas. I had allowed myself to be pulled by the same temptations that pull most people in the world—relationships, validation, approval, and the desire to be loved in ways that were not always healthy or wise.

That did not mean God abandoned me. But it did mean I was walking in territory where the enemy had more room to operate.

The devil's goal has never changed. Jesus describes him plainly: the thief comes "to steal, kill, and destroy" (John 10:10). If he cannot destroy someone through direct attack, he will try to lead them into choices that weaken the protection they once walked under.

The story never ends with temptation.

Because the moment someone turns back toward God, the enemy's strategy begins to unravel. That return is possible because of what Jesus accomplished. Through Him, repentance and forgiveness open the door for restoration. What once separated us from God can be confessed, released, and forgiven. The path back is never closed.

That is exactly why the enemy works so hard to prevent repentance.

Jesus describes Satan plainly as a thief: "The thief comes only to steal and kill and destroy" (John 10:10). The enemy's goal is always loss—stealing hope, destroying relationships, and turning pain into isolation. But Scripture also contains an interesting principle about thieves. Proverbs says that when a thief is caught, he must repay what he stole many times over—sevenfold (Proverbs 6:31).

The enemy knows that principle well. If he can keep someone trapped in shame, bitterness, or self-blame, the theft stays hidden. But the moment someone turns back toward God, the thief is exposed. What was stolen can be reclaimed. What was meant for destruction can be redeemed.

That is why the enemy works so hard to keep people away from God. Shame becomes louder. Fear becomes heavier. Self-blame grows stronger. Anything that convinces a person to stay hidden, isolated, or condemned serves his purpose. Because as long as someone believes they cannot return to God, the enemy does not have to fight them—he has already convinced them to stay away.

For years that strategy worked on me. After my daughter died, grief, fear, and guilt became walls between me and God. I blamed myself. I replayed every decision. I carried wounds that were never meant to be carried alone. In many ways I hid from God the same way Gideon hid in the winepress—believing that staying small and unseen was the safest place to be.

The enemy never fears your hiding. He fears your return. Because the moment someone turns back toward God, the thief is caught—and the process of restoration begins.

It took me a long time to understand that this pattern wasn't unique to my story. It's woven all through Scripture. From the beginning, the enemy's strategy has always been the same: if he cannot curse what God has blessed, he tries to lure it away from God instead.

That realization helped me see something deeper about the nature of spiritual attack. What Balaam exploited in Israel wasn't a new trick—it was a pattern that goes all the way back to the very beginning.

Here's the clearest way I can say what finally clicked for me—shaped by what I heard from Rabbi Manis Friedman and Rabbi Ted Falcon, and then tested in Scripture and in my own life.

In Eden, the tree of the knowledge of good and evil wasn't hidden in a corner; it stood "in the middle of the garden" (Genesis 2:9). Choice was built into the center of the story. Not because God wanted Adam and Eve to fail, but because love without freedom isn't love. To give real freedom, God (who is righteous and just) honors His own word. That means He doesn't rig the game. He doesn't smother the choice. He lets a real "no" be possible, even while He's whispering a better "yes."

Revelation pictures the enemy "thrown down to the earth" (Revelation 12:9). However you parse the timeline, the point is this: the serpent was allowed to speak. And Adam was innocent. Too innocent to even know what "protect yourself" meant. They hadn't tasted evil or death. They were newborns asked to choose trust in a world where a liar could still talk. Scripture even hints at the world God intends by painting scenes where predator and prey live at peace—the wolf with the lamb, the leopard with the young goat, the lion eating straw like the ox, and "they will not hurt nor destroy" on God's holy mountain (Isaiah 11:6-9; 65:25, WEB). That shalom backdrop makes the intrusion of the serpent feel all the more jarring: a voice of rupture entering a creation designed for harmony.

Is that a fair fight? No. The devil "prowls around like a roaring lion, seeking whom he may devour" (1 Peter 5:8). He aims at innocence. He loves untaught gates. And that, strangely, is the first answer to "why does God allow attack?" Because He made us image-bearers with agency, and agency has to be trained. God will defend; God will deliver; but God will also dignify you—teach your hands to war (Psalm 144:1), grow your discernment, and form courage that can't be counterfeited. He doesn't fight Satan as our substitute *in the practice of daily choices*—He already crushed the serpent's head in Christ (Genesis 3:15; Colossians 2:15). Now He teaches us to stand in that victory: "Resist the devil, and he will flee from you" (James 4:7). It's not God vs. a co-equal god. It's the Creator who has already won, training His children to enforce the win.

God answers—not with a lecture but with a name. "Yahweh is with you, you mighty man of valor," He says to Gideon while Gideon is hiding in a winepress (Judges 6:12). God calls him what he is in God's plan while he still feels like what he isn't in his own skin. And God doesn't remove the battle—He shrinks the army so Gideon will learn the exchange: your weakness for My strength—"The people who are with you are too many... lest Israel boast" (Judges 7:2). Valor isn't the absence of fear; it's obedience inside of it.

That tracks with my story more than I wish it did. As a young adult I was Anna-from-*Frozen*—in love with being in love. I thought I could inspire people into goodness, and the world taught me otherwise—pregnant at 19, single mother at 20, learning the hard line between what's lovely and what's true. If we're going to carry real freedom, we end up *learning* the difference between good and evil the costly way—not just as information, but as formation. The enemy exploits that gap; God uses it to grow a spine.

So why does God allow attack?

- Because love requires real choice. The tree in the middle means your "yes" matters—and so does your "no."
- Because courage must be formed. Innocence is beautiful, but it isn't yet battle-tested. God fathers you into wisdom.
- Because He's not absent; He's training. He has already judged the serpent; now He teaches you to stand, speak, and shut the gates (Ephesians 6:10–18).
- Because He meets you in weakness. "Yahweh is with you" *while you're hiding*. He calls you valor before you feel it, and then He proves it with you, not just for you.

If you're asking, "But why *this* much pressure?"—welcome to Gideon's field and Mary's flight. When the Seed is planted, Herod hunts (Matthew 2). Hell tries to kill what heaven conceives. That's not proof you heard wrong; sometimes it's proof you heard right. The answer isn't to muscle through in self-will. It's to keep trading your weakness for His strength, your panic for His pace, your guesses for His word—until the voice in your chest sounds less like the serpent and more like the Shepherd (John 10:27).

Promise, Inheritance, and the Story of Abraham

Once I began to understand why spiritual attack happens, another question naturally followed: if God allows testing and training, how does anyone keep going through it?

Scripture shows that God rarely sends people into a difficult journey without first giving them a promise. Not a vague encouragement or motivational slogan, but a real promise about what He intends to do. Those promises act like landmarks in the distance. You may not be able to see the entire path yet, but you know the direction you are walking.

One of the clearest examples of this pattern appears in the story of Abraham.

When God first speaks to Abraham, nothing about his circumstances suggests that he is about to become the father of a nation. He is already advanced in age, and his wife Sarah is barren. From a human perspective, the future God describes seems impossible. Yet God speaks with certainty: "I will make of you a great nation… and in you all the families of the earth will be blessed" (Genesis 12:2–3).

That promise arrives long before its fulfillment.

Years pass. Decades even. Abraham walks through uncertainty, waiting, mistakes, and difficult decisions. At times the promise seems so delayed that Abraham and Sarah attempt to solve the problem themselves, creating complications that ripple through the rest of the story. Yet throughout those long years God continues repeating the same assurance: a son will come, and through that son a people will be born.

The promise comes first. The inheritance comes later.

In the language of Scripture, the promise reveals purpose. It points toward what God intends to do through a person's life in His kingdom. The inheritance, however, reveals something deeper. It speaks to what someone receives simply because they belong to God.

For Abraham, the promise was that his life would become a blessing to nations. But the inheritance was not merely land or descendants. It was covenant. It was relationship with God Himself. Scripture later describes Abraham not only as the father of many nations but as a friend of God. Long before the promise fully unfolded, Abraham was already walking in the deeper gift of that relationship.

This pattern still appears in the lives of those God calls today. When the Holy Spirit begins drawing someone into a new direction, He often gives a glimpse of kingdom purpose before the journey fully begins. That glimpse becomes an anchor during seasons when the road feels uncertain or slow. The promise reminds you that the journey is not random and that God sees a destination even when you cannot.

At the same time, the inheritance remains present throughout the entire journey. God's delight in His children is not postponed until the promise is fulfilled. It exists from the beginning. The relationship itself is part of the inheritance.

Without the promise, the training can feel pointless. Without the inheritance, the journey can feel lonely. But when both are understood together, the path begins to make sense. God is not only shaping what we will eventually do; He is shaping who we are becoming as His sons and daughters.

Like Abraham, we learn to walk forward step by step, trusting that the God who called us also delights in us along the way.

The Adventure of Manifesting with the Holy Spirit

Walking with the Holy Spirit has felt, at times, like bootcamp. Not the kind of bootcamp where you just learn a skill and move on—but one where every muscle of the soul is tested, stretched, and strengthened. Ascension isn't all soaring light and heavenly visions. Sometimes it has meant sitting in the ashes like Job, staring at the wreckage of my life and asking the hard question: *Why me? Why this?*

And the Holy Spirit wouldn't let me run. Not into distractions. Not into numbing myself with unhealthy coping mechanisms. Instead, He taught me to sit with my emotions and feel them, raw and unfiltered. To let grief wash over me. To face my fears instead of burying them. That part wasn't fun—it burned. But fire always purifies, and slowly I learned that even my tears were part of His refining.

Yet this journey has also been an adventure. There were days I felt like a character in a movie, looking around and wondering: *Is anyone else seeing this?* Signs, synchronicities, prayers answered in impossible ways—things so miraculous they felt like magic. But it wasn't magic. It was the Holy Spirit weaving heaven into the fabric of my everyday. Ordinary days became vibrant, full of color and meaning. Even the hard parts became bearable because I wasn't carrying them alone.

That's the missing piece when people try to manifest without the Holy Spirit. Science can explain energy, thought patterns, and biology, but Dr. Dispenza and Dr. Lipton leave out the mystical reality: without the Holy Spirit, manifestation is striving; with Him, it becomes surrender and wonder.

Maybe you've been trying to live life in your own strength, hustling, grinding, striving—and still finding yourself empty. I've been there. I've burned out more times than I can count. But what I discovered is that with the Holy Spirit, I am no longer carrying life alone.

Which is why, six months later, when God told me it was time to leave the job he brought me because I outgrew the environment, I still panicked. I had responsibilities. I was raising my sister's three children. Hustling and grinding was how I thought I had to survive. I even bargained with God: *Maybe if I get fired, I can at least collect unemployment.* But I realized that wasn't faith—that was me trying to cling to a safety net.

So in July 2025, trembling but determined, I quit. No backup plan. No net. Just His word and the promise of this book.

I wish I could say I floated on a cloud of faith after that, but the truth is I felt like I was free-falling. My mind raced: *I need to grow my YouTube channel, build my TikTok, hustle harder, market this book.* It was Plan G, Plan H, Plan I. The backup plans never ended. And through all my scrambling, God whispered the same word: *Rest.*

Rest? I thought. How do you rest when the world demands hustle? When your family already thinks you've lost your mind? I had lived this way since 2010: outworking everyone, hustling in survival mode, and still never being given a chance. No one bet on me. No one believed in me. No one... except God.

And then it clicked. Just as I had realized I couldn't fake surrender by hoping for unemployment, I also couldn't cling to the world's way of striving. I remembered what I had declared back in October 2024: *I tried life the world's way. I tried life my way. Now I only want to live life God's way. Take the wheel, Jesus.*

Maybe God is asking you to do something that feels just as impossible. To let go. To step out. To trust Him when you'd rather cling to control. If so, I can tell you this: the free fall won't destroy you. Because you're not falling—you're being held.

That is the Holy Spirit.

And that is when I realized my mind had been renewed. Renewal isn't pretending the old fears don't exist; it's unlearning their impact. It's letting the subconscious be reprogrammed by truth instead of trauma. The viruses of fear, insecurity, and shame were being overwritten by love, hope, and courage because the kingdom of heaven is within us.

This is what manifesting with the Holy Spirit feels like. Not escaping reality, but living it more fully. Not magic, but miracle. Not striving, but surrender. And the adventure isn't over—it's still unfolding, one day, one breath, one act of trust at a time.

The same Holy Spirit who carried me through will meet you, too—closer than your breath, ready to walk with you into your own story of fire, refining, and wonder.

Chapter Three

Authority, the Serpent, and the Fall

It began in the garden. Not with a bite, but with a whisper.

The serpent leaned in close to Eve, not with force, but with suggestion: "Did God really say…?" (Genesis 3:1). The deception landed in her mind before it ever reached her hand. Sin did not begin when she bit into the fruit — it began when agreement was forged in her thoughts. The deception landed in her mind before it ever reached her hand. When she looked at the fruit and decided it was "good for food" and "desirable to make one wise" (Genesis 3:6), the agreement was already forged. Sin did not begin when she bit into the fruit — it began when she entertained the thought, accepted the doubt, and aligned her desire with the lie. That inner dialogue of doubt, inadequacy, and suspicion was the crack in the door through which death entered.

That's where the real war begins: in the mind. Eden was not just a garden, it was alignment itself—a sacred state where humanity walked in unbroken harmony with God. The tragedy of the fall was not simply that paradise was lost, but that the harmony of mind and spirit with heaven was fractured. Ever since, the mind has been the gateway of agreement.

Manifestation always begins in the mind. Before anything takes shape in the visible world, it is first conceived in thought, belief, and imagination. This is why negative self-talk matters so much: it doesn't just affect mood or confidence — it shapes the very atmosphere of your spirit and the direction of your life.

And this is why attempts to manifest without the Holy Spirit — through affirmations, vision boards, sound baths, or even sophisticated therapies — can only reach so far. They may reprogram the conscious mind temporarily, but they cannot uproot the ancient wound of sin. The root problem is not simply psychological; it is spiritual. And only the Spirit of God can cut that deep.

Without the Holy Spirit, you can only polish the surface. With the Holy Spirit, you are transformed from the inside out.

The Serpent and the Nature of Deception

If negative self-talk begins with agreement, then we need to look closely at the very first deceiver. Who was the serpent in Eden?

The Bible simply calls him "more subtle than any animal of the field which Yahweh God had made" (Genesis 3:1). But layers of tradition and Scripture hint that this was no ordinary snake.

Scripture shows that Satan did not fall alone. "His tail drew one third of the stars of the sky, and threw them to the earth... and his angels were thrown down with him" (Revelation 12:4, 9). Peter and Jude echo the same reality: "God didn't spare angels when they sinned" (2 Peter 2:4);

"angels who didn't keep their first domain... he has kept in everlasting bonds" (Jude 6).

Ezekiel uses throne-room imagery to describe a figure as "the anointed cherub who covers," walking "among the stones of fire" before iniquity was found in him (Ezekiel 28:14-15). Many Christian readers take this as a typological window into Satan's pre-fall rank—a cherub. In scripture, cherubim are awe-inducing, multi-faced, multi-winged guardians of God's presence—attending His throne, bearing His chariot, veiling themselves in reverence, and moving at the Spirit's command (Genesis 3:24; Exodus 25:18-20; Ezekiel 1; 10; Revelation 4).

Seraphim (Hebrew *sĕrāphîm*, from *śāraph*, "to burn") are "burning" heavenly beings seen "above" God's throne with six wings—two covering the face, two covering the feet, and two for flight—crying, "Holy, holy, holy is Yahweh of Armies" (Isaiah 6:2-4). One touches Isaiah's lips with a live coal to purify him (Isaiah 6:6-7). The Hebrew word *seraph* also means "fiery serpent" in other passages (Numbers 21:6; Isaiah 14:29; 30:6), which is why some traditions imagine a serpentine, flaming aspect; still, Isaiah 6 is our clearest seraphim scene. Related throne-room "living creatures" in Revelation also have six wings and sing "Holy, holy, holy" (Revelation 4:6-8).

Because the Hebrew word seraph can also mean "fiery serpent" (Numbers 21:6; Isaiah 14:29; 30:6), some traditions imagine a seraphic/serpentine aspect around Eden's deception. Scripture doesn't rank angels, but later Christian tradition often places seraphim at the top of angelic orders, with cherubim just beneath.

Therefore, aside from Ezekiel, I believe scripture suggests that the enemy was a seraph. Nonetheless, if Satan was a high-ranking cherub, he may have then enlisted a seraph to embody the serpent because after all, Satan, a fallen throne guardian (depicted as a cherub in Ezekiel's language), rebelled and drew other angels into his fall (Revelation 12:4, 9). The Eden tempter is identified with him. Nonetheless, any further link to a seraph is an interpretive possibility, not a biblical certainty.

Why does this matter for manifesting with the Holy Spirit? Because if Eve saw only an animal, she might have been guarded. But if she saw a radiant being, an angel of light, she would not have felt threatened. The Apocryphon of Eve (though not Scripture) reflects this idea, portraying the serpent as more than a beast. Secondly, Jewish scholar Efraim Palvanov notes that some Kabbalists also believed Eve was speaking to a light-being. Paul warns us that "Satan masquerades as an angel of light" (2 Corinthians 11:14). The serpent was not merely crawling on the ground—it was deception cloaked in familiarity, beauty, even glory.

And what was the serpent's strategy? Not force, but suggestion. Not a demand, but a whisper. The same whisper that still echoes in our minds today: *"You are not enough. You are lacking. You could be more."*

God's first question to humanity after the fall strikes at the heart of this: "Who told you that you were naked?" (Genesis 3:11). In other words: Who told you that you were lacking? Who told you that what I gave you wasn't enough?

This is the essence of negative self-talk. It is not just psychological—it is spiritual deception. It begins as a suggestion, a seed of doubt, planted in the mind. And the moment we agree with it, it takes root.

The Kinsman Redeemer

Sin doesn't change who God is, but it changes where we stand. "Your iniquities have separated between you and your God" (Isaiah 59:2). Separation is not the Father's desire; it's the inevitable consequence of violating holiness. From Eden on, the wage attached to sin is death (Romans 6:23). If the wage is life, then only life can answer it.

That's why Scripture keeps pointing us to blood—not as superstition, but as God's appointed sign of life poured out. "For the life of the flesh is in the blood... I have given it to you on the altar to make atonement for your souls" (Leviticus 17:11). Blood says: a real life has stood in for the guilty. Redemption is costly; it is never paid with ideas, only with life.

Israel's law made this visible. The nearest male relative—the kinsman-redeemer (go'el)—had the duty to buy back what was lost, rescue kin from slavery, and keep the family name from being erased (Leviticus 25:25, 47-49; Deuteronomy 25:5-10). The story of Ruth shows how this works in flesh and blood: a qualified kinsman who is near enough, able, and willing steps forward to redeem (Ruth 3-4). But even Israel's sacrifices and best obedience could only point beyond themselves. "It is impossible that the blood of bulls and goats should take away sins" (Hebrews 10:4). The law exposed our need; it could not cure the disease (Galatians 3:24; Romans 3:20).

So God did what love does: He drew near as family. "When the fullness of the time came, God sent out his Son, born to a woman, born under the law, that he might redeem those who were under the law" (Galatians 4:4-5). The Son took "flesh and blood" so that "through death he might bring to nothing him who had the power of death" (Hebrews 2:14-17). He entered our story as the true Kinsman—of David's royal line according to the flesh (Romans 1:3; Luke 1:32-33)—to do what Israel's priesthood and sacrifices could only foreshadow: pay the full price with His own blood. "In whom we have redemption through his blood, the forgiveness of our trespasses" (Ephesians 1:7). Heaven sings it plainly: "You purchased us for God with your blood" (Revelation 5:9).

This is why we come to the Father through Jesus. He is not one more pathway; He is the Kinsman with the receipt. "I am the way, the truth, and the life. No one comes to the Father, except through me" (John 14:6). "God so loved the world, that he gave his one and only Son... that whoever believes in him should not perish, but have eternal life" (John 3:16). The distance sin created is closed not by sentiment, but by substitution—a life given for life, a blood-sealed covenant that opens the door and keeps it open (Hebrews 10:19-22).

So when you feel far, remember what closeness cost. The distance you sense is precisely what the Kinsman came to cross. Your access isn't fragile; it is blood-bought. Come again by the living way He opened (Hebrews 10:19-22). Confess, and be cleansed (1 John 1:9). Lift the cup of the new covenant and remember: the life is in the blood, and His life has been poured out for you.

Head First

When sin entered the world, God called out to Adam first: "Where are you?" (Genesis 3:9). Responsibility begins at the head. Adam was meant to guard, to cover, to protect—but when his guard was down, the enemy's whisper slipped past. Pastor Jerry Flowers, Jr. of Redefined TV, says it plainly: the battle of sin started in the mind, and that's where God always begins His work.

This is why the veil in the temple was torn from the top down when Jesus died on the Cross (Matthew 27:51). Transformation begins in the head—in thought—before it moves down into behavior. We often want to go "feet first," focusing on changing habits and actions, but God starts with the head. He knows that unless the mind is renewed, the feet will keep walking in circles.

Paul echoes this truth: "Don't be conformed to this world, but be transformed by the renewing of your mind" (Romans 12:2). The mind is the gateway. Agreement happens in thought before it becomes action. Negative self-talk, fear, and doubt—all are whispers waiting for your agreement. And agreement is powerful enough to shape your reality.

This is why manifesting without the Holy Spirit will always fall short. You may train your behavior, repeat affirmations, or try to "think positive," but without the covering of Christ's blood and the renewing of the Spirit, the root lies in place. Manifestation without God is feet-first. Manifestation with the Holy Spirit is head-first.

The Holy Spirit meets us at the top, breaking chains in the mind before they ever reach the hand. He silences the serpent's whisper and replaces it with the Father's voice: "You are mine. You are loved. You are chosen."

Agreement and the Power of Thought

In Eden, as previously mentioned, the sin was not just in the consuming—it was when Eve looked at the fruit, agreed with the idea, and then gave it to Adam. But notice this: sin did not enter the bloodline when Eve ate—it entered when Adam did. Adam was the head, the one charged with protecting her, yet his guard was down. By his agreement, death entered humanity's bloodstream.

Agreement is powerful. The thoughts we choose to align with don't just float away; they shape our reality. Modern science confirms what Scripture has told us from the beginning: "As a man thinks in his heart, so is he" (Proverbs 23:7).

Science now helps us glimpse how this is possible. Gregg Braden, a New York Times best-selling author, researcher, and speaker notes that the Human Genome Project, completed in 2003, shocked researchers: instead of the 100,000 genes they expected, humans have only about 20,000–25,000—roughly the same as a worm. The missing "complexity" isn't in the DNA sequence but in how those genes are expressed. Dr. Bruce Lipton's research in epigenetics shows that gene expression is shaped by environment, belief, and thought. In other words, the subconscious programming we inherit—including trauma, fear, and patterns of sin—gets written into us before we're even born.

This makes Genesis startlingly relevant. Just as sin entered Adam's bloodline, science shows how ancestral patterns can echo through generations. What we call "generational curses" Scripture identifies as the sins of the fathers visiting the children (Exodus 20:5)—and epigenetics shows how this can literally manifest in the body through gene expression.

Consider pregnancy. Lipton's research demonstrates that how a mother is treated during pregnancy shapes the subconscious programming of the fetus. A father's love, support, and protection don't just impact the woman emotionally—they influence the biology of the child she carries. A father's absence, neglect, or rejection plants seeds of insecurity in the unborn child's subconscious. When the father abandons his role, stress floods the mother's body, and that chemistry programs the developing child with fear, insecurity, or anger.

And here is the heartbreaking reality of modern life: just as Adam failed to protect Eve, many fathers fail to protect women today. Studies show that in the United States, about 40% of all births are to unmarried women (CDC, 2023). In some communities, that number climbs even higher. To make matters worse, welfare programs of past decades often penalized families if the father was present in the home, creating an environment where men were pushed out rather than drawn in. Satan has always targeted fathers because he knows that if he can undermine the head, the whole body suffers.

This is why the birth of Jesus is also so significant. As I established earlier, He was born of the seed of a woman, not of man. Therefore, His blood was not tainted by Adam's curse. His bloodline was holy, unbroken, unstained. That's why His sacrifice as the Lamb of God is enough to cover the blood of Adam—and yours, too as our Kinsman Redeemer.

Furthermore, notice Joseph's role. When Mary was pregnant, Joseph could have rejected her. By law, she could have faced public disgrace, even death. But Joseph chose to protect her. He accepted Mary, accepted the child, and in doing so, reflected the heart of the Father. Imagine how deeply that must have comforted Mary in her pregnancy. And when she visited her cousin Elizabeth, even Elizabeth's unborn son leapt in recognition at the presence of the Messiah (Luke 1:41). Two fetuses, already reacting in spirit, affirm that what happens in the womb matters profoundly.

This is why His sacrifice as the Lamb covers us. His blood answers for Adam's sin. His obedience overturns Adam's agreement. Just as the veil of the temple was torn from top to bottom, God begins His redemption with the head first—the mind, the place where agreement is forged.

And this is why Communion is so vital. When we eat of His body and drink of His blood, we remain under His covering. Jesus said, "Whoever eats my flesh and drinks my blood remains in me, and I in them" (John 6:56). In Communion, we participate in the reversal of Eden—we agree not with the serpent's lie, but with Christ's life. We take into ourselves the blood that saves, the body that heals, and we declare with our whole being: my agreement belongs to Jesus.

Communion is also a training ground for manifesting with the Holy Spirit. When we receive the bread and the cup, we do more than follow ritual—we activate imagination and faith. Catholics often describe this as truly eating His body and drinking His blood, and their faith allows them to experience healing, renewal, and breakthrough through this act. That is the power of belief and imagination aligned with God's promise. It is the same principle at the root of manifestation—but here, it is sanctified. Instead of projecting self-will, we are aligning our will with God's, literally taking Christ into ourselves as the substance of our agreement.

In Communion, we practice the very essence of manifesting with the Holy Spirit: picturing, believing, receiving, and embodying God's Word until it becomes reality. The bread and cup train us to imagine His covering as real, to agree with His blood over our bloodline, and to manifest His life in our bodies and spirits.

In Adam, sin poisoned the bloodline. In Jesus, blood became redemption. His holy blood covers the curse, breaks the chain, and writes a new inheritance for those who believe.

Manifesting Without the Holy Spirit

Manifestation always begins in the mind, but without the Holy Spirit, it never reaches its true destination.

The world offers many tools—affirmations, vision boards, sound therapy, even meditation practices borrowed from Eastern traditions. These can bring some results, but they cannot touch the root of the problem. At best, they polish the surface; at worst, they open the door to deception.

Why? Because the foundation is missing. Without the Holy Spirit, manifestation operates from the broken programming of original sin. Negative self-talk—*"I'm not enough, I'll never succeed, I don't deserve love"*—is not just a bad habit. It is the echo of Eden, the serpent's whisper reverberating through generations. Left unchallenged, that programming sets the tone for a person's subconscious, shaping thoughts, beliefs, and even the body itself.

Dr. Joe Dispenza and others have shown that focused thought and imagination can change neural pathways and create new patterns of behavior. But here's the hidden variable: who are the people in those studies? They are often individuals who have the money and freedom to attend high-cost retreats, people not deeply trapped in generational trauma or poverty. If their starting point is already privileged, of course their results will appear dramatic. But what about those born into trauma? Those whose subconscious programming was written in pain before birth?

And this is why manifesting without the Holy Spirit is incomplete. It attempts to rewrite the script without addressing the Author. It seeks to create without the Creator. Without Christ's blood covering the bloodline of Adam, without the Spirit renewing the mind, manifestation cannot break the chains of original sin.

The enemy knows that when we agree with his lies, even unintentionally, we hand him access. That's why negative self-talk is so powerful—it's agreement in disguise. The serpent didn't force Eve to eat; he planted a thought, and she agreed. Adam agreed as well, and sin entered the bloodline. In the same way, every time we agree with lies about our worth, identity, or future, we echo that first deception.

But here's the difference: with the Holy Spirit, we don't just reframe our thoughts; we break the agreement. We cover our bloodline with the blood of Jesus. We stop being victims of programming and become temples of the living God.

How Agreement Affects Our Inheritance

As a consummate explorer and author of Birthright, Timothy Alberino points out, when we give agreement to lesser beings, we forfeit inheritance. Agreement is never neutral—it either aligns us with God's order or hands over our birthright to the deceiver.

According to this view, every human inherits the right to govern Earth as a birthright from Adam. Dominion over creation was not given only to the righteous or earned through merit; it was woven into humanity's very design. As the sons and daughters of Adam—made in the image of God—we were appointed to stand as regents, representing His seal on earth.

History confirms this truth. Leadership and governance have not been limited to the virtuous. From kings and emperors to presidents and rulers, both good and corrupt, humanity has exercised dominion across the world. The right to govern is not earned by personal achievement—it is inherited. It flows through the bloodline of Adam, embedded in our very genome, a reflection of the divine legacy placed on humanity itself.

What God gave by inheritance, the enemy has always sought to corrupt through agreement. The Book of Enoch describes how the Watchers, angelic beings, longed to take what was not theirs. They descended to earth, took human wives, and taught forbidden knowledge, producing offspring—the Nephilim. These hybrids were outside of God's design, a corruption of humanity's inheritance. When the flood came, their bodies perished, but their spirits remained, condemned to wander the earth as unclean spirits.

The lesson is sobering: anything outside of God's creative will cannot inherit heaven.

Fast forward to today. We live in an age of transhumanism—the attempt to merge humanity with technology in order to "upgrade" what God has designed. Companies are developing brain-machine interfaces, implantable chips meant to merge thought with artificial intelligence. Biohackers promise genetic edits that will erase disease or enhance abilities. To many, it sounds like progress. But at its core, the question is the same as in Eden: *Did God really say?* Is His image not enough?

Scripture teaches that we were made in God's image and sealed with His Spirit (Ephesians 1:13). If the enemy cannot erase that seal, he will attempt to counterfeit it. Just as the Watchers corrupted flesh in ancient days, transhumanist visions seek to alter the blueprint of humanity. If we rewrite God's image in ourselves—whether through genetic manipulation or merging with machines—we risk creating something God did not intend, something that cannot bear His seal.

And this is where the spiritual stakes rise. If thought itself is the battleground, what happens when the battlefield is wired to a machine? Whose voice speaks through a brain chip? Whose influence flows through reprogrammed DNA? These technologies may not look like demonic giants, but the spirit behind them is the same: a rebellion against the God who formed us.

This is why we must be discerning. Not every innovation is evil, but when technology tempts us to reject God's design in pursuit of our own, it echoes the Watchers' ancient rebellion. The same scheme repeats today. The enemy whispers lies, tempting us to give our agreement to thoughts of fear, inadequacy, and rebellion. Each time we agree with the serpent's suggestion, we surrender ground that was meant to be ours in Christ. But in Jesus, the Second Adam, the inheritance is restored. His blood covers the corruption of Adam's seed, breaking the enemy's legal claim and reestablishing our rightful place as heirs with Him (Romans 8:17).

The Courtroom of Heaven

Satan is a legalist. He knows the rules, and he twists them against us. His strategy is not just temptation but litigation—he accuses, argues, and uses our very words and thoughts as evidence against us. Scripture shows Satan accusing (Job 1:6–11; Zechariah 3:1), and names him "the accuser of our brothers... who accused them before our God day and night," yet declares his defeat "because of the Lamb's blood" (Revelation 12:10–11).

Even Adam and Eve, who knew no sin, tasted death by agreeing with him. God had warned them, "You shall surely die," but death only entered once sin did. How could they have grasped the full weight of their choice? This reveals a sobering truth: in the courtroom of heaven, ignorance does not nullify agreement. You don't have to fully understand what you are consenting to in order for it to hold up in Heaven's court.

This is why the Holy Spirit's presence in our lives is indispensable. He is not only Comforter but Counselor—the One who warns us, convicts us, and guides us so we don't unknowingly give consent to lies. Without His help, we would be defenseless against an accuser who has studied humanity for millennia.

Scripture gives us a vivid picture of this courtroom reality. Daniel describes: "I watched until thrones were placed, and one who was ancient of days sat. His clothing was white as snow, and the hair of his head like pure wool. His throne was fiery flames, and its wheels burning fire. A fiery stream issued and came out from before him. Thousands of thousands ministered to him. Ten thousand times ten thousand stood before him. The judgment was set, and the books were opened" (Daniel 7:9–10).

The book of Job confirms this cosmic courtroom scene: "Now on the day when God's sons came to present themselves before Yahweh, Satan also came among them" (Job 1:6). The accuser still seeks opportunity to build his case against God's people.

The psalmist writes, "God presides in the great assembly. He judges among the gods" (Psalm 82:1). And

Revelation shows us the final verdict: "I saw a great white throne, and him who sat on it, from whose face the earth and the heaven fled away... I saw the dead, the great and the small, standing before the throne, and they opened books. Another book was opened, which is the book of life. The dead were judged out of the things which were written in the books, according to their works" (Revelation 20:11-12).

But here is our hope: Jesus now stands as our Advocate. He is the greater Adam who did not fail, the One whose blood answers every accusation. In the heavenly courtroom, where the accuser presses his charges, Christ intercedes on our behalf. And the Holy Spirit testifies within us, leading us into truth and sealing us as heirs of the promise.

Without Jesus and the Holy Spirit, we cannot stand. With them, the verdict is settled: forgiven, redeemed, covered in the blood of the Lamb. This is why manifesting without the Holy Spirit is dangerous—it leaves us vulnerable in the courtroom. But manifesting with Him places us under Christ's advocacy, where every lie is silenced and every accusation answered.

Parasitic Power

"Vampires" are folklore, but the picture works: parasitic evil living off the life of others. Good needs no host—God is self-existent: "I AM" (Exodus 3:14). Deception can't sustain a kingdom—"If Satan has risen up against himself... he can't stand, but has an end" (Mark 3:26). Fallen spirits cannot create life; they hijack life through human agreement and defilement.

Scripture names the levers:
- **Accusation and twisted Scripture**: the adversary accuses (Zechariah 3:1; Revelation 12:10) and quotes the Bible out of context (Matthew 4:6).
- **Consent and participation**: "You are servants of whoever you obey" (Romans 6:16). "What they sacrifice, they sacrifice to demons... You can't partake of the Lord's table and of the table of demons" (1 Corinthians 10:20-21).
- **Blood-guilt defiles places**: "They shed innocent blood... the land was polluted with blood" (Psalm 106:37-38; cf. Numbers 35:33).
- **Footholds**: "Don't give place to the devil" (Ephesians 4:27).

Yes, "the life of the flesh is in the blood... to make atonement" (Leviticus 17:11). But the life of the spirit must be in the mind, hence why the battlefield of the spirit is the mind: "take every thought captive" (2 Corinthians 10:5). Agreements are signed first in thought.

How did the enemy get this leverage? There is no clear answer to this, but it makes me wonder if in fact the enemy did it on purpose. He rebelled and was cast down. Jesus said, "I saw Satan having fallen like lightning from heaven" (Luke 10:18); Revelation names him "the great dragon... thrown down to the earth" (Revelation 12:9).

After the fall, he works as "the prince of the power of the air" (Ephesians 2:2) and "the whole world lies in the power of the evil one" (1 John 5:19)—not by rightful title, but by usurped influence through human agreement, worship, and blood-guilt. He rages because "he knows that he has but a short time" (Revelation 12:12). Does that mean he knows he has a short time to amass power?

God answered the initial legal problem of sin entering human blood with a kinsman redeemer's blood. "When the fullness of the time came, God sent out his Son, born to a woman, born under the law, that he might redeem those who were under the law" (Galatians 4:4–5). The Son took our flesh and blood (Hebrews 2:14–17) and redeemed us through his blood (Ephesians 1:7), canceling the record and disarming rulers and powers (Colossians 2:14–15). That's why we come to the Father through Jesus (John 14:6).

Now please take this next part back to God as it is my hypothetical theory. Picture this, though, evil "feeds" on humans to temporarily remain in existence; similar to the temporary blood sacrifice of animals; evil's influence grows where we agree.

Aaron Abke writes in his book, *The Three Beliefs of Ego: A Sufferer's Guide to Freedom*, that those determined to be evil are still only doing what they believe to be good for themselves, even if it is not good for others. Therefore, if we look at motives, such as Satan wanting to be like God or greater, this implies that he purposely tainted humans with sin to be cast down to the earth. Becoming its prince was intentional. To maintain existence, the enemy "sacrifices" as many human souls as possible in a twisted form of spiritual atonement which may explain how he can still have access to Heaven's court to accuse us, and why he and demons are constantly taking our grievances to God.

Nonetheless, the more sin he collects, the more it separates him from God, the more he has to devour to remain in existence. However, he and the angels he took with him had to think it were possible to overthrow God if they were willing to take such a risk knowing God is all mighty and all powerful.

Secondly, the "Watchers" in the Book of Enoch married human women who bore them "The Nephilim.... Those were the mighty men who were of old, men of renown" (Genesis 6:4). In 1 Enoch 7, it says that when the giants ran out of food, "they turned against [humans] and devoured mankind," then even drank blood. Jubilees 7 echoes that the giant clans began destroying and devouring humans and each other.

Long story short, after Jesus defeated the enemy on the cross, the only thing left for him to do is obtain your agreement. Therefore, this is just another reason to remain in alignment with God by manifesting with the Holy Spirit. Shut the doors in the mind and at the table. Renounce lies (2 Corinthians 10:5). Refuse divided loyalties (1 Corinthians 10:21). Keep no foothold (Ephesians 4:27). Worship God (Matthew 4:10). And stand in the finished verdict of the blood.

The Power of Our Words: A Double-Edged Sword

The importance of our voice cannot be overstated. Even God created the cosmos by speaking: "And God said, 'Let there be light,' and there was light" (Genesis 1:3). Creation itself is a testimony that words carry weight, shaping reality.

Scripture never treats words as neutral. James warns: "The tongue is a small member, yet it boasts great things. See how a small fire can spread to a large forest!" (James 3:5). John's vision of Christ in Revelation shows Him with a sharp two-edged sword proceeding from His mouth (Revelation 1:16). The image is deliberate: His Word is not sentimental poetry—it is a weapon of truth, cutting through deception. Hebrews reinforces this: "For the word of God is living and active, and sharper than any two-edged sword, piercing even to the dividing of soul and spirit" (Hebrews 4:12).

Our words, too, carry this double edge. When spoken, written, or even muttered under our breath, they enter the atmosphere as frequencies. Negative self-talk doesn't disappear—it imprints on our subconscious and reinforces the lies of the enemy. This is why self-centered manifestation collapses: words spoken apart from heaven's authority lack eternal power. Word's spoken without the love and redemptive power of Christ don't transform a person's belief about themselves when they have been rehearsing the enemy's lies all their life.

Without the Holy Spirit, we are vulnerable to channeling lesser spirits. These entities may disguise themselves as benevolent guides, but the truth is sobering: any spirit that draws attention away from God and claims our voice commits idolatry with us. How "good" can a spirit be if it knowingly participates in rebellion against the Creator?

As previously discussed, according to The Book of Enoch, when God destroyed the world with the flood, the Nephilim's physical bodies perished, but their spirits remained—disembodied, wandering the earth without rest because they were never part of God's design. These spirits crave influence and, above all, a human voice. Channeling, then, is not harmless—it is the surrender of your God-given authority to voices that were never meant to exist. The moment you give them your attention, you open the door for the enemy to gain a foothold.

This is why manifesting with the Holy Spirit is the only safe and true way. He does not usurp your voice—He indwells, empowers, and aligns it with heaven. Instead of forfeiting inheritance to deceivers, you receive your rightful inheritance as a child of God.

But when surrendered to God, your words become instruments of creation. Aligned with the Holy Spirit, they harmonize with God's blueprint. Just as Jesus wields the sword of His Word, you too wield a voice sharpened by truth. With it, you bless, build, heal, and manifest heaven on earth.

Choosing Your Agreement

The point is simple but weighty: you are important. You are powerful in your own right, and that power makes you both influential and vulnerable. Every person must decide—will you be an instrument of God, or a tool of the devil?

The devil works through deceit. "He was a murderer from the beginning, and doesn't stand in the truth, because there is no truth in him... he is a liar, and the father of lies" (John 8:44). His whispers become negative self-talk, the relentless inner critic that repeats: You're not enough. You're unloved. You're unworthy. These thoughts don't vanish into thin air—they sink into the subconscious, shaping belief, emotion, and even genetic expression. He whispers lies, manipulates agreement, and twists truth to gain access to your voice, your mind, and your inheritance.

Science confirms what Scripture has been saying all along. Researchers like Dr. Lipton show that thoughts and beliefs can literally switch genes on or off—a process known as epigenetics. Subconscious programming often begins in the womb, influenced by the emotional environment of the parents. No wonder Scripture says, "The fathers have eaten sour grapes, and the children's teeth are set on edge" (Ezekiel 18:2). Generational curses are not only spiritual but can be biological—patterns written into the body itself.

Affirmations, vision boards, even therapy are meant to be tools and can be very helpful. Sometimes God will work through other people. I know they are helpful because I have tried all of them. Vision boards help one to remain positive and hopeful. Affirmations remind people to endure. And Therapy gives your pain a voice in order for it to be released.

However, it is a very tedious and lengthy task to rewrite the programming of the subconscious all on your own. Without the Spirit of God, we are left battling a subconscious already coded by generations of fear, shame, and brokenness which some people describe as past lives. That is why so many attempts at self-driven manifestation fail to bring lasting fruit.

God, on the other hand, never forces Himself. He waits at the door. Jesus said, "Behold, I stand at the door and knock. If anyone hears my voice and opens the door, then I will come in to him, and will dine with him, and he with me" (Revelation 3:20).

This is why agreement is everything. Just as Adam and Eve's agreement with the serpent opened the door to sin, so your agreement—whether conscious or unconscious—determines whose voice you amplify in your life. Satan will gladly take your silence, your passivity, or your careless words as consent. But God, in His love, will only move when you invite Him.

That invitation is twofold. We must invite Jesus to return as King at the end of days—"The Spirit and the bride say, 'Come!'... Yes, come, Lord Jesus" (Revelation 22:17, 20)—and we must invite the Holy Spirit into our own temples daily. "Don't you know that your body is a temple of the Holy Spirit who is in you, whom you have from God?" (1 Corinthians 6:19).

I learned this personally in October 2024. My entire journey with what I now call Ascension Bootcamp did not begin until I spoke aloud and invited the Holy Spirit in while watching Dee's YouTube video. That was the pivot. That was the moment heaven met me in my weakness and began reshaping everything from the inside out.

The same is true for you. Your voice carries eternal weight. "Death and life are in the power of the tongue" (Proverbs 18:21). Your invitation opens the door. The choice is yours: whose agreement will you live under?

Chapter Four

Guarding the Gates of the Mind

As we've seen in Chapter Two, the great conflict between good and evil plays out first in the unseen realm of thought. Your mind is the gate of agreement. What you dwell on, what you permit, what you align with determines the atmosphere of your spirit. Victory or defeat begins not with outward behavior, but with inward agreement.

The psalmist echoes this truth: "Lift up your heads, you gates! Be lifted up, you everlasting doors, and the King of glory will come in" (Psalm 24:7). In Scripture, city gates represent authority and decision—what enters and what is kept out. Spiritually, your mind and senses serve as those gates.

This is why attention matters. What you give attention to, you give permission to. The enemy cannot read your mind, but he does whisper—and he thrives on agreement. Not every thought that passes through your mind is yours. Some are prompted by the Holy Spirit, others are broadcast by the enemy, and some arise from your own processing. Discipleship is learning to discern the difference.

So imagine yourself as a watchman at the city gate—or like Heimdall on the rainbow bridge in the movies—sword in hand, deciding what may pass. That's what it means to guard your mind: not generating every thought, but testing every thought. The world calls some people "psychic," but often they are simply more aware that thoughts can come from outside. What the world distorts, Scripture redeems. God designed prophetic sensitivity as a gift for communion with His Spirit (1 Corinthians 12:28). The gift is real; the source and agreement determine whether it is holy or harmful.

Discerning Your Own Thoughts

If there are God's thoughts and the enemy's thoughts, then how do I know which ones are mine? That's a fair question, especially if you are just beginning to hear the voice of God. It can feel unsettling when you realize some of the thoughts you always assumed were "yours" may have been enemy broadcasts all along. And when you start discerning between the two, it may feel like you're caught in a cosmic tug-of-war, swallowed up in the battle between good and evil.

And that is exactly what the enemy wants you to feel: powerless, small, and uncertain. But God wants you to know the opposite—that you are unique, chosen, and full of purpose.

Scripture affirms this over and over:
- "I praise you, for I am fearfully and wonderfully made" (Psalm 139:14).
- "Before I formed you in the womb, I knew you. Before you were born, I set you apart" (Jeremiah 1:5).
- "Now you are the body of Christ, and members individually" (1 Corinthians 12:27).

God gave you a mind, a voice, and a personality that are uniquely yours. Your own thoughts are not the enemy—they are your God-given capacity to discern, to question, to process, and to choose.

Here's how it works:
- God inspires thoughts aligned with truth, love, and peace.
- The enemy broadcasts whispers of fear, shame, or despair.
- Your thoughts are the space of discernment—the inner voice that listens, weighs, and decides which to agree with.

Paul says, "Take every thought captive to the obedience of Christ" (2 Corinthians 10:5). That doesn't mean every thought is evil; it means you have authority to decide what stays and what goes.

Think of this life as training ground. In the physical world, thoughts do not always manifest instantly, but they still carry energy. In near-death experiences, many report that in the spiritual realm, everything is telepathic—whatever you think becomes reality instantly. That's why it's so important here and now to practice aligning your thoughts with God. If your imagination and energy are trained in agreement with His Spirit, then your manifestations flow with heaven's order.

The enemy is not all-knowing. He cannot see into your mind the way God can. But he studies patterns—your body language, tone, and reactions. And he has many lesser spirits at his disposal, broadcasting lies in hopes you'll mistake them for your own thoughts. His strategy is to plant suggestions, wait for you to agree, and then accuse you for them.

But the Holy Spirit gives you a different path. Manifesting with the Holy Spirit is not about erasing your individuality, but about discovering who you are without sin. It is learning to peel back the layers of deception, shame, and false agreement so that your authentic self—the one God designed—can emerge in purity and power.

With Him, your true self is not swallowed by the battle, but revealed, empowered, and aligned with God's glory.

So when you hear the voices swirl, remember: your thoughts matter. They are not erased by the Holy Spirit—they are refined, renewed, and given the power to manifest heaven on earth.

Thoughts as Energy

Energy is at the heart of this conversation. Scripture says, "God is light, and in him is no darkness at all" (1 John 1:5). Modern science, in its own way, affirms that everything in creation reduces down to energy and light. Einstein's famous equation, $E = mc^2$, reveals that energy and matter are not separate but different expressions of the same reality.

Think of it this way: mass is energy slowed down and condensed, while light is energy moving unimaginably fast. One is heavy, structured, and particle-like; the other is fluid, radiant, and wave-like. Together, the equation shows that "slow energy" multiplied by "fast energy squared" equals the total energy of the universe. In 1997, physicists at Stanford

Linear Accelerator Center even demonstrated the creation of matter from light by colliding high-energy photons—confirming what Scripture has declared from the beginning: light and life are inseparably woven together.

The human body is no exception. Both the brain and the heart generate measurable electromagnetic fields that extend beyond the body itself. These fields interact with the environment around us, shaping and being shaped by it. The holographic principle in physics suggests that information once thought confined to one place—like the brain—can actually be distributed across a system. Likewise, memory, intelligence, and impressions appear to be encoded throughout the nervous system, not just localized in one organ.

This helps explain why some thoughts feel like they come from outside us. Psychoanalyst Carl Jung described this as the collective unconscious—a shared reservoir of human thought and archetype. Science is beginning to catch up. In Spontaneous Evolution, Dr. Lipton and Steve Bhaerman highlight evidence that collective thought patterns exist and can influence not only society but even biology.

Modern research also points to this mystery. Dr. Dispenza's work on neuroplasticity shows that focused thought can reshape brain pathways and raise the body's frequency, even producing measurable healing. And yet, here discernment is vital: science can explain the mechanics, but it cannot redeem the soul. Without the Holy Spirit, we remain bound by trauma, sin, and the density of the flesh. Only the Spirit can clear blockages, heal wounds, and align us with heaven's frequency.

Paul explains it this way: "If the Spirit of him who raised up Jesus from the dead dwells in you, he who raised up Christ Jesus from the dead will also give life to your mortal bodies through his Spirit who dwells in you" (Romans 8:11). And again: "We all, with unveiled face, beholding as in a mirror the glory of the Lord, are transformed into the same image from glory to glory, even as from the Lord, the Spirit" (2 Corinthians 3:18).

This is true ascension—not escaping yourself into a void, but being transformed into your truest self in Christ. What some call quantum jumping or even science fiction imagines as time travel, Scripture describes as the Spirit lifting the soul into higher states of being through union with God.

In short: thoughts are energy, but not all energy leads to life. When aligned with the Holy Spirit, your thoughts vibrate with heaven's frequency and manifest God's reality on earth.

The Observer Effect and Intrusive Thoughts

What are intrusive thoughts? Intrusive thoughts are unwelcome, disturbing, or random ideas that seem to appear out of nowhere. They often carry fear, shame, accusation, or despair. Many people assume these thoughts reveal something dark inside themselves—but this is not the case. Recognizing them as broadcasts rather than your own creation helps lift the weight of guilt. Not every thought in your head is "yours."

The enemy knows this. He broadcasts whispers and accusations, hoping you will take ownership of them. But the truth is: a thought only gains power when you agree with it. When you give attention to an intrusive thought, you collapse its potential into reality. Remove your agreement, and the thought loses its power.

This is where the observer effect from modern physics gives us a helpful picture. In quantum mechanics, particles like electrons or photons don't remain in one fixed state until they are observed. Before observation, they exist in a wave of possibilities. The moment attention is given, the wave collapses into one definite outcome. In other words: observation changes reality.

Spiritually, the same principle applies. Jesus said, "According to your faith be it done to you" (Matthew 9:29). Faith, belief, and imagination are forms of attention—they direct your spiritual sight. Attention is the observer effect of the soul: what you behold, you help bring into reality.

This explains why trauma, unforgiveness, or heavy emotions like anger, depression, guilt, and shame make us feel "dense." They collapse us into fixed patterns, like particles bound by weight. But forgiveness, worship, and union with the Holy Spirit lift us into the freedom of possibility, like waves of light. The Holy Spirit used these principles to show me deeper biblical mysteries. For instance, I came to understand that Jesus was able to walk on water because His very being vibrated at a higher frequency—His body resonating with the glory of heaven rather than the density of earth. Scripture records: "In the fourth watch of the night, Jesus came to them, walking on the sea" (Matthew 14:25). Similarly, Enoch and Elijah were both taken up without tasting death—a picture of lives lifted beyond the weight of this world's density. Many who return from near-death experiences describe Earth as one of the "heaviest" realms of creation, noting that re-entering their body feels restrictive compared to the lightness of the spiritual dimension.

In Jesus, what was impossible for the particle became natural for the wave.

So what do we do with intrusive thoughts? We don't suppress them, because fear feeds them. We don't agree with them, because agreement gives them power. Instead, we let them pass through us like waves, without collapsing them into particles. And we actively redirect our attention through Christ.

James adds: "Resist the devil, and he will flee from you" (James 4:7).

Here's a simple pattern for dealing with intrusive thoughts:

- **Notice it** – Pause and recognize: "I see this thought."
- **Name it** – Don't own it. Say: "This is not from God."
- **Resist it** – Speak aloud: "I rebuke this thought in the name of Jesus. By His blood, I reject this lie and command it to leave."
- **Replace it** – Declare Scripture or truth. Example: if the thought says, "You are worthless," reply, "I am fearfully and wonderfully made" (Psalm 139:14).
- **Invite peace** – Pray: "Holy Spirit, fill my mind with Your peace and truth. Silence every other voice but Yours."

Thoughts are like visitors at the door—you decide who enters.

And when you do this consistently, you begin to rewire the gates of your mind. Intrusive thoughts stop defining you. The Holy Spirit clears old blockages and creates a steady flow of peace, joy, and clarity. Sometimes battles lift quickly; other times, they persist. If intrusive thoughts become overwhelming or impact daily functioning, seeking help from a trusted pastor, counselor, or doctor is not a lack of faith—it is often the very way God provides healing through others.

Priests as Bridges: Ushering Heaven to Earth

In the ancient world, priests stood in the gap between heaven and earth. They carried the prayers of the people before God and brought God's blessing back to the people. Scripture affirms this calling for every believer: "You are a chosen race, a royal priesthood, a holy nation, a people for God's own possession" (1 Peter 2:9). To be a priest means to be a bridge—to join heaven and earth through worship, intercession, and agreement with God's will.

But no human priest could fully restore what was broken in Eden. That is why Christ came. "We have a great high priest who has passed through the heavens, Jesus, the Son of God" (Hebrews 4:14). Jesus is the ultimate bridge—the one who tore down the veil, reconciled us to the Father, and poured out the Holy Spirit so that heaven could dwell within us.

When you manifest with the Holy Spirit, you are stepping into this priestly role. You are not pulling reality from thin air or bending the universe to your will. You are joining your faith, imagination, and words to God's Spirit, allowing His reality to flow through you into the earth. This is what Jesus meant when He taught us to pray: "Your kingdom come, your will be done, on earth as it is in heaven" (Matthew 6:10).

Think of it this way: Adam and Eve were the first priests in Eden, walking in alignment with God and tending the garden as a sacred space. Sin fractured that alignment. But Christ, the Second Adam, restores it. Through Him, we once again become priests—our lives, minds, and words becoming altars where heaven touches earth.

To manifest with the Holy Spirit, then, is to carry out this priestly calling. Every prayer you lift, every word of truth you speak, every act of love you choose is like incense rising before God's throne. And every time you surrender your imagination and voice to the Spirit, you help usher His kingdom into visible reality.

Jesus is the High Priest who mended the bridge. The Holy Spirit is the living presence that flows through it. And you, as a royal priest, are invited to stand on that bridge—bringing heaven to earth with every agreement you make with God's truth.

Priests at the Gates: Manifesting through Sacrifice

Father Mike Schmitz once preached that if you are baptized, then you are already a kingdom priest. Priests, by their very design, exist for worship—and at the heart of worship is sacrifice. The very word "worth-ship" implies that what you are willing to sacrifice reveals what you genuinely believe is worthy.

Scripture reminds us, "You also, as living stones, are built up as a spiritual house, to be a holy priesthood, to offer up spiritual sacrifices acceptable to God through Jesus Christ" (1 Peter 2:5). If we sacrifice time, comfort, or resources for entertainment, that becomes what we ascribe worth to (idols). If we sacrifice in obedience and love to God, then He is revealed as our ultimate worth.

Keith Guiles expressed this truth profoundly when he said, "God would rather die than live without you." And in Christ, He did just that. Jesus is the High Priest, the one mediator between God and humanity due to original sin. Ministerial priests unite their prayers to Jesus during the liturgy, while kingdom priests—every baptized believer—are called to unite their prayers with the ministerial priest. Paul writes, "I appeal to you therefore, brothers, by the mercies of God, to present your bodies a living sacrifice, holy, acceptable to God, which is your spiritual service" (Romans 12:1). This means that when the Eucharist is offered, we too are meant to place something on the altar: our struggles, problems, fears, and burdens from the week. Our sacrifices—imperfect as they may be—are gathered up into Christ's perfect sacrifice.

At its root, the word sacrifice means "to make sacred." What we lay down in faith—our time, our fears, our desires, our struggles—ceases to be ordinary when offered to God. They are transformed into holy offerings because they are placed into His hands. As Paul reminds us, "For everything created by God is good, and nothing is to be rejected, if it is received with thanksgiving. For it is sanctified through the word of God and prayer" (1 Timothy 4:4–5). In this way, even the most painful or mundane parts of our lives can become sacred acts of worship when surrendered at the altar.

This truth—that sacrifice makes the ordinary sacred—prepares us to understand the blood of the Lamb. Rabbi Kirk Schneider points us back to Exodus, where the blood of the lamb painted on the doors became the mark of protection during Passover. "They shall take some of the blood, and put it on the two door posts and on the lintel, on the houses in which they shall eat it" (Exodus 12:7). In Revelation, Jesus is called the Lamb of God twenty-eight times, fulfilling that same promise of deliverance and covering. "Worthy is the Lamb who has been killed to receive the power, wealth, wisdom, strength, honor, glory, and blessing!" (Revelation 5:12).

Today, we paint the blood of Jesus on the gates of our mind, heart, and home—not with hyssop on wood, but through Holy Communion, through prayer, and through picking up our cross daily as royal priests in God's Kingdom. Jesus said, "If anyone desires to come after me, let him deny himself, take up his cross, and follow me" (Matthew 16:24).

The Counterfeit of Babel and the Truth of Identity

The story of the Tower of Babel sets the stage for one of the greatest misunderstandings about manifestation. In Genesis 11, humanity united with one goal: "Let's build ourselves a city, and a tower whose top reaches to the sky, and let's make a name for ourselves" (Genesis 11:4). Their ambition was not evil in appearance—it was unity, progress, and achievement. But the heart behind it was. Their goal was independence from God. They sought to reach heaven without Him, to claim purpose apart from the Creator.

God intervened by scattering the people and their cultures, breaking the illusion of self-sufficient ascent. The tower reminds us that manifestation rooted in human pride may look promising but ultimately leads to division, confusion, and collapse. Babel was not just a tower—it was a mindset that persists whenever we treat human knowledge as self-sufficient, divorced from the Creator.

Case in point, our modern culture teaches us to separate science from faith, as if they occupy opposite ends of reality. This false divide has become one of the enemy's most effective footholds. By divorcing our beliefs from our practices, we lose sight of how God's truth is meant to touch every dimension of life—from how we think and eat, to how we heal, create, and connect. When science is divorced from worship, it becomes a tower of Babel; but when united under Christ, it becomes a testimony of His wisdom woven into creation.

In other words, thought is not only personal—it is energetic, relational, and transmissible. Some thoughts are whispered into our gates by God's Holy Spirit, others are injected as warfare by the enemy, and still others emerge from our own inner processing. But they all flow through a medium of energy, and that energy interacts with our hearts, minds, and even our biology.

Modern science offers us a striking parallel in the cosmic microwave background—the faint afterglow of the universe's beginning. Physicists describe it as the oldest light still resonating through creation, a whisper from the dawn of time that fills every corner of space. It is subtle but ever-present, carrying information about the birth of the cosmos itself.

In the same way, our thoughts, prayers, and even unspoken desires carry resonance, as in Jung's collective (un)consciousness. They ripple outward, shaping not only our own lives but the spiritual atmosphere around us. Just as the cosmic microwave background reveals that creation itself began with a burst of divine speech—"God said, 'Let there be light'" (Genesis 1:3)—so too does every word and every thought reveal its source, carrying energy that either aligns with light or distorts it.

Guarding one's thoughts, renewing the mind, and practicing protective measures are considered enduring principles in Scripture, with some interpretations drawing parallels to modern physics by highlighting the connection between thought and energy and the importance of monitoring one's mental patterns.

As watchmen at the gates, we are not merely individuals fending off stray thoughts—we are priests standing guard over a sacred temple. Peter reminds us, "You are… a royal priesthood…" (1 Peter 2:9). To be part of this priesthood means we carry the responsibility of discerning what enters the temple gates of mind, heart, and spirit. A priest does not live for himself alone; he mediates between heaven and earth, offering sacrifices that keep the people aligned with God. Likewise, when we guard the gates, we are not simply protecting ourselves but also cultivating an atmosphere where God's Holy Spirit can flow outward for the good of others.

Modern science, interestingly, has begun to rediscover fragments of this truth. Researchers like Dr. Dispenza have documented how meditation can produce profound effects on the brain, body, and even measurable healing. His findings on neuroplasticity and the ability to rewire thought patterns through focused meditation, once again, echo back to Romans 12:2, "Be transformed by the renewing of your mind". Dispenza shows us that thoughts and emotions influence biology, and that meditation can unlock resilience and wholeness in ways medicine is only beginning to understand.

Here lies the danger: Dr. Dispenza often teaches that the path to manifestation and healing requires a surrender of the self, even the erasure of identity—losing yourself into nothingness in order to access everything. At first, this may sound like humility, but in truth it mirrors the error of Babel. Once again, in Genesis 11, humanity sought to ascend by erasing dependence on God, uniting around their own self-made path to heaven. The pursuit of becoming "no one" to become "everyone" is not freedom—it is an echo of Babel's self-sufficient illusion.

The gospel, by contrast, does not erase the self; it redeems it. Christ does not call us to lose ourselves into a void but to discover our true selves in Him—the selves He created, loved, and redeemed. Manifestation with the Holy Spirit is not about escaping identity but about aligning identity with divine purpose.

This is where Simon Sinek's insights on leadership and organizational culture are revealing. He has shown that what drives people is not money or status but meaning—the why behind what they do. Companies that fail to provide a sense of purpose collapse from within, just as surely as Babel did. People long for purpose because it is written into our design. Here is the key distinction: when purpose is cut off from the Creator, it eventually corrodes into burnout, exploitation, and emptiness. When purpose is rooted in God, it becomes life-giving not only to the individual but also to the community.

The royal priesthood does not stand as blank slates but as consecrated vessels. We manifest not from nothingness, but from fullness—the fullness of Christ who dwells within us. When we meditate, it is not to dissolve the self but to walk alongside in harmony with God's Holy Spirit. True manifestation flows not from the erasure of "I am" but from agreement with the Great I AM.

Spiritual Warfare

Scripture exhorts us: "Put on the whole armor of God, that you may be able to stand against the wiles of the devil" (Ephesians 6:11). Paul describes this armor in detail (Ephesians 6:13–18), and each piece has a spiritual function:

- **The Belt of Truth** (v. 14) – fastens everything together. When lies attack, declare God's Word over your situation. Speak truth aloud: "I am chosen, loved, and redeemed."

- **The Breastplate of Righteousness** (v. 14) – guards the heart. You are covered not by your own goodness, but by Christ's righteousness. Remind yourself: "I am in right standing with God through Jesus."
- **The Shoes of the Gospel of Peace** (v. 15) – give firm footing. When anxiety or chaos rise, stand in God's peace: "My steps are ordered by the Lord, and He gives me peace that passes understanding."
- **The Shield of Faith** (v. 16) – deflects and extinguishes fiery darts (intrusive thoughts) of doubt, fear, and accusation. Lift it by declaring your trust: "I choose to trust God's promises, not the enemy's lies."
- **The Helmet of Salvation** (v. 17) – protects the mind. Cover your thoughts with the truth of your salvation: "My mind is guarded by Christ; I belong to Him."
- **The Sword of the Holy Spirit** (v. 17) – the Word of God, used offensively. Speak Scripture directly against lies, just as Jesus did in the wilderness. For example, when fear attacks, say: "God has not given me a spirit of fear, but of power, love, and a sound mind" (2 Timothy 1:7).
- **Praying in the Holy Spirit** (v. 18) – constant communication with God, inviting His presence into every moment.
- You can "put on" the armor daily through prayer.

This is where our power of belief and imagination becomes essential. Paul tells us to put on the armor. That means we don't only recite it—we visualize it, believe it, and embody it.

The mind's eye is not just fantasy—it's a God-given faculty. When you imagine yourself fastening the belt of truth, or raising the shield of faith, you are training your spirit to align with reality. Neuroscience shows that visualization activates many of the same neural pathways as physical action. A study in 1994 of subjects visualizing piano exercises activated neural pathways in the motor cortex similar to them physically performing the exercises. Spiritually, the principle is the same: where your attention goes, energy flows.

If your attention lingers on intrusive thoughts, they grow stronger. If your attention fixes on Christ and His promises, that is where spiritual energy flows. This is why Paul exhorts us: "Set your mind on the things that are above, not on the things that are on the earth" (Colossians 3:2).

From Babel's Illusion to God's Manifestation

In this way, manifestation is no longer about extracting reality for ourselves but about becoming vessels through which God's reality flows. "For we are his workmanship, created in Christ Jesus for good works, which God prepared before that we would walk in them" (Ephesians 2:10). We manifest for others, and we receive what God provides for us. Our individuality, far from being erased, is preserved and redeemed—because in the kingdom of God, every priest has a special purpose. Each sacrifice becomes a thread woven into the greater tapestry of His glory.

So when you put on the armor of God, it is not just symbolic—it is participatory.

- **Believe it** (faith activates it).
- **Visualize it** (see it in your mind's eye).
- **Focus on it** (direct attention toward it so energy flows into it).
- **Speak it** (release it into reality through the Word).

And when intrusive thoughts arise, this is where the observer effect becomes spiritual:

- Notice the thought.
- Refuse to own it.
- Rebuke it in Jesus' name.
- Redirect your attention to Scripture or a Spirit-filled image of truth.

What you focus on grows. Where you place your belief and imagination directs the flow of spiritual energy. And when that attention is fixed on Christ, you align with the true Source of power.

This is the posture of true manifestation with the Holy Spirit. Not striving to bend reality for personal gain but surrendering to the Holy Spirit so that God's life flows through you. Each time you believe, imagine, focus, and speak, you are not building Babel's tower—you are embodying heaven's temple. Your life becomes a living sacrifice, a vessel of glory, a priesthood in service of the King.

Chapter Five

Jesus' Hero's Journey and Ours

Every culture tells stories of heroes: called to adventure, tested by trials, descending into darkness, and finally returning transformed. Joseph Campbell called it the monomyth—the hero's journey that underlies myths across the world. But with Jesus, this pattern is not myth. It is history. He embodies the hero's journey in flesh and blood. And unlike mythic heroes, His story is not just an inspiring tale—it is the blueprint for our own transformation.

Before the call to adventure comes, one's soul aches for something more. That ache shows up as longing, desire, or a deep restlessness that whispers, *There must be more than this.* This is where prayer begins—not as ritual words, but as the soul reaching for God.

Gregg Braden describes what he calls the "lost mode of prayer," suggesting that something vital was left out of our modern translations of Scripture. Ancient Hebrew prayer carried not just words but *feeling*—the embodied gratitude and joy of the prayer already answered. Jesus pointed to this when He said: "Therefore I tell you, all things whatever you pray and ask for, believe that you receive them, and you shall have them" (Mark 11:24). Belief is not mere thought—it is experienced in the heart, held as already true.

I learned this truth in my own way. One night, I sat in the dark with my eyes closed and imagined holding a seed in one hand and digging the earth with the other. I named the seed—my hope, my desire, my dream—and then I placed it into the soil and covered it. It was an act of surrender, but also of faith. By imagining the seed already planted, I was embodying what Braden calls the lost mode of prayer: holding the vision, feeling the gratitude, and entrusting the growth to God.

For example, if I prayed for a house, I would see myself gardening, blessing the land, and creating nourishment from the soil. If I asked for a job, I would imagine myself leading with integrity and compassion. If I sought provision to pay off my bills, I would feel the freedom of serving my community with time and energy released. The desire was never just for me—it was always connected to God's Kingdom.

This is where the hero's journey meets Kingdom manifestation. The Call to Adventure is not only the naming of desire—it is the soul's yes to step beyond the ordinary world into God's extraordinary purpose. Gratitude becomes the soil, faith the water, and the Holy Spirit the light. The seed is not ours to force—it is His to grow. And as Jesus showed at Lazarus' tomb, even before the miracle came, He lifted His eyes and thanked the Father (John 11:41–42). That is the lost mode restored: prayer as gratitude, surrender, and faith embodied.

When we walk with the Holy Spirit, our struggles, longings, and wilderness seasons fall into this same divine pattern. In Christ, the story written into creation becomes personal: descent becomes ascent, shadow becomes light, and desire—sown in faith—becomes the harvest of new life.

The Call to Adventure

The Hero's Journey always begins with a descent—into the soil, into the womb, into the waters of the unknown. Jesus Himself said, "Unless a grain of wheat falls into the earth and dies, it remains by itself alone. But if it dies, it bears much fruit" (John 12:24). A seed must first die to the soil before it can rise into the light. A baby must leave the safety of the womb before entering the world. A dragonfly larva must leave the waters of its birth to take flight in the air. A caterpillar must enter the cocoon, dissolving into stillness before emerging transformed.

So too with the Hero. The call to adventure is a call to descend into the collective unconscious—the world of symbols and fragments. Here the hero meets the broken pieces of self, mirrored in supporting characters. For Jesus, the disciples were not just companions but facets of humanity's story: impetuous Peter, doubting Thomas, zealous James and John, betraying Judas. They represented the fragments of the human soul He carried with Him on the journey.

Jesus' first sign—the wedding at Cana where He turned water into wine—was such a call. It was not merely about saving a feast, but about answering the invitation into His mission. Wine flowed in place of water, joy from purification, transformation from the ordinary. It was the first seed planted, a foreshadowing of the greater work to come.

And in the soil of the seed, the womb of the mother, the waters of the larva, and the cocoon of the butterfly lies the same truth: God uses hidden places to refine, prune, and prepare us. The wilderness is where He does His deepest work—unseen, but not wasted.

Jesus' journey began not with fanfare but in the waters of the Jordan. Though He was without sin, He stepped into the river where sinners confessed their failures. His descent was not into guilt but into solidarity—identifying fully with humanity's wounds and shadows.

Water has always symbolized the unknown and the hidden depths. In Scripture, it represents both chaos and cleansing: the flood that covered the earth, the Red Sea Israel passed through, the mikveh baths of ritual purification. Jung described water as an archetype of the collective unconscious—the deep reservoir where humanity's myths, fears, and longings reside.

By immersing Himself in the Jordan, Jesus descended into the shared depths of the human soul. And at that moment of descent, heaven broke open. The Holy Spirit descended like a dove, and the Father's voice declared, "This is my beloved Son, with whom I am well pleased" (Matthew 3:17). In the language of myth, this was the supernatural aid, the Mentor appearing. In truth, it was the Holy Spirit empowering Him for the journey to come.

Threshold Crossing

From the Jordan, Jesus was led into the wilderness. The wilderness is always a place of stripping—where comfort, security, and false support fall away. For forty days, He fasted. The adversary whispered, "If you are the Son of God..." (Matthew 4:3).

The temptation was not about bread or kingdoms. It was about identity. Would He prove Himself through spectacle and trust the Father's word alone? In the wilderness, He was stripped down to the core: Who am I? What is my purpose?

I know this stripping well. In 2015, when my daughter passed away, my identity collapsed into tragedy. Five years later, after leaving my long-term relationship and the two stepsons I had helped raise, I found myself alone in a small apartment during the pandemic, walking my dogs through the silence of Bear Creek Lake Park.

Who was I outside of grief? Outside of being "the mother who lost a child"? My life felt like it had collapsed into a single, painful story. Like Jesus in the desert, I was forced to confront the core question: Who am I, really?

In that wilderness season, suicidal thoughts pressed in. Cabin fever gave way to derealization. I knew if I stayed still, I might not survive. So I packed my car with my dogs and drove into the unknown. The road became my wilderness. From Colorado to Georgia to Florida and back again, I wandered, burdened with limerence, running with fearful-avoidant attachment issues, weighed down with perseverative intrusive thoughts, and carrying PTSD like desert burdens.

However, just as manna fell in the desert, God left me signs along my own wilderness path. I would find business cards tucked into snow covered branches at Bear Creek with verses like "All things work together for good" (Romans 8:28) and "Cast your burden on the Lord, and He will sustain you" (Psalm 55:22). Crosses on churches caught my eye from the road. Billboards lit up with Jesus' name as if heaven itself was breaking into neon.

Jung spoke of archetypes—universal patterns etched into the human soul. Campbell mapped them into the hero's journey. Underhill described them in mystical stages. Scripture itself is filled with archetypes: the serpent of deception, the lamb of sacrifice, the shepherd as guide, the bride as the people of God.

I began to notice synchronicities that were too precise to be coincidence. A verse appearing exactly when I needed it. A song lyric echoing a hidden prayer. My Bible app opening spontaneously while I drove. These weren't glitches—they were guidance.

The world might call this "the universe sending signs." But Scripture says: "The anointing which you received from him remains in you... his anointing teaches you concerning all things" (1 John 2:27). Synchronicities are not random—they are the Spirit's way of confirming, nudging, and directing.

One night on the road, traveling from Missouri to Tennessee, I typed the address of my hotel into the GPS. But when I arrived, the destination had somehow shifted—I wasn't at the hotel, but at a gas station. I felt prompted to go inside, wondering if there was something for me there. At first nothing stood out, but I thought: *if there is a sign, it will be in the pop section,* (because pop has always been my favorite thing). Sure enough, there it was. An entire refrigerated wall filled with Coke bottles, every label facing forward—except for the one in the center. Its message: *"Share a Coke with a Hero."*

These were not coincidences. They were wilderness whispers: *You are not forgotten. This stripping is preparation because there is more still to come.*

It took three years of being in the wilderness before I was even close to being ready for my Cherith season, of what I call God's ascension bootcamp. From the time I was running around the country in the Ghostland of the pandemic, I eventually had to re-enter the working world in 2021. I ran into a marriage I just as quickly had to run out of only six months later. That year brought with it a diagnosis of rheumatoid arthritis. I had to juggle changing medications—not only for the pain and inflammation in my body but also for PTSD, searching for some combination that could keep me functioning. By December, I finally surrendered to the idea of doing intensive outpatient group therapy.

At the beginning of 2022, in one of those therapy sessions, my counselor finally spoke the one truth that reverberated through my shock, grief, trauma, and wandering in the unconscious—something everyone else seemed too afraid to say: *"Jesus died on the cross for our sins so that you don't have to go through hell. You don't have to go through the underworld or the abyss to save your daughter because Jesus already did."*

If there has ever been a moment when I could consciously feel chains shattering and strongholds breaking off, that was it.

Nonetheless, even then, the wilderness didn't end. I still had to pick myself up and keep going. After my sister passed in 2020, I walked through the long legal and financial maze in 2022 to gain guardianship of her children when they needed a forever home—never knowing how I would pay for the next step.

I tried and failed, got up, brushed myself off, tried again, failed, got up, brushed myself off, and tried again more times than I can count. That is the key to endurance: keep getting back up. Keep walking forward in blind faith. Again, three years, rarely seeing more than one step ahead, and never knowing how God was going to provide. But He did provide. He did keep me afloat.

I want to make it be known: the stripping, while necessary to your hero's journey and ability to later manifest with the Holy Spirit, is not going to be easy. Don't give up. Take a moment, have a meltdown, and then get back up.

It may not take the same length of time for some people, but I want to be honest about the timeframe. These chapters may move quickly on the page, but in real life the wilderness can feel as if it drags on. That's why I structured the book this way: to give you a sense of the whole process, but also to serve as markers you can return to. Each chapter is meant to meet you in whatever season you find yourself, to remind you what's happening, what to expect, and how to endure it.

Trials and Sacrifice

Jesus' ministry, too, was marked by trials: rejection, confrontation with darkness, betrayals, misunderstandings, demands for signs. Each test prepared Him for the Cross.

- **Rejection in His hometown:** When Jesus returned to Nazareth and read from Isaiah in the synagogue, the people who had known Him since childhood turned against Him. They were enraged, drove Him out of town, and even tried to kill Him (Luke 4:28-30). Rejection prepared Him for the greater rejection He would face at the Cross.
- **Temptation in the wilderness:** After His baptism, the Holy Spirit led Him into the desert to face the adversary. For forty days He was tempted with hunger, power, and glory (Matthew 4:1-11). Each time He stood firm in God's Word, foreshadowing His ultimate obedience in Gethsemane.
- **Confrontation with religious leaders:** Again and again, the Pharisees and Sadducees demanded signs, tried to trap Him with questions, or accused Him of blasphemy (Matthew 12:38; 22:15-18). Their hostility sharpened His resolve and revealed the depth of opposition He would endure.
- **Misunderstanding by His followers:** Even those closest to Him struggled to grasp His mission. At times the disciples argued about greatness (Mark 9:34), rebuked Him when He spoke of suffering (Matthew 16:22-23), and fell asleep during His most agonizing

prayer (Matthew 26:40). Their weakness mirrored the loneliness He would carry on the Cross.

- **Betrayal by Judas:** One of the twelve He had chosen handed Him over for thirty pieces of silver (Matthew 26:14–16, 47–50). The sting of betrayal by a friend pierced His heart and prepared Him for the weight of bearing the world's sin.
- **Denial by Peter:** The disciple who swore he would never abandon Jesus denied even knowing Him three times before the rooster crowed (Luke 22:60-61). The pain of denial showed the cost of human weakness—and the depth of forgiveness Jesus would extend through the Cross.

Each of these trials was part of His preparation. None were wasted. Together they formed the path of obedience that led Him to Calvary, shaping Him as the forerunner of our own journeys through testing and surrender.

The Many Become One

In prayer, I was once taken back to the moment before Jesus died on the Cross. I saw a line of people stretching through history, and I was among them. No one present at Calvary could see us, yet we were there—all of humanity drawn together in that hour. One by one, we stepped into Him, each assuming His posture as He hung from the wood.

When He cried out, "My God, my God, why have you forsaken me?" (Matthew 27:46), He wasn't alone. We were with Him, sharing in His cry. That was the moment we all collapsed into Him. Our grief, our sin, our death—released with His final breath. The Cross was not only His descent into the abyss; it was ours as well.

Paul describes this mystery: "I have been crucified with Christ, and it is no longer I who live, but Christ lives in me" (Galatians 2:20). Again he writes, "Our old self was crucified with him, that the body of sin might be done away with" (Romans 6:6). My vision was a glimpse of that truth—the many becoming one in Him, every life gathered into His sacrifice so that every life might also share in His resurrection.

Campbell and Jung observed that in the Hero's Journey and the collective unconscious, the hero encounters fragments of himself in the supporting characters. The end of the journey is integration—the gathering of scattered pieces into wholeness. I often hear people speak of "integrating the shadow," and there is truth in this; when suppressed, the shadow twists and distorts. But deeper still, it is the shards of light that must be gathered. Jewish Kabbalists describe these as sparks of divine light fractured from the beginning, scattered throughout creation, waiting to be returned to God. In much the same way, our own lives are fractured by suffering and sin, yet each shard retains its own identity and brilliance. The path of wholeness is not the loss of self, but the restoration of these pieces in Christ.

For years I wrestled with the New Age concept of oneness, which seemed to blur individuality into sameness. Why would I be "fearfully and wonderfully made" (Psalm 139:14) if my distinct soul, my voice, and my story were only illusions? Over time, in prayer and reflection, I came to see that the longing behind oneness—the ache for connection—was not wrong. What is wrong is the erasure of individuality. The truth is more beautiful: interconnectedness without loss of self, harmony without uniformity.

This is why your individuality matters. In Christ, you are not erased, but fulfilled. The Holy Spirit does not flatten us into sameness; He weaves us into harmony. As Paul reminds us, "Now you are the body of Christ, and members individually" (1 Corinthians 12:27). Each of us carries a unique gift, a thread that, when woven with others, forms the living tapestry of Christ's body.

In daily life, this looks like honoring the strengths and perspectives of those around you. When you encourage someone's voice, you participate in the Spirit's work of unity. When you forgive, pursue healing, or step into your calling, you add your note to the greater song of Christ's body. Jesus prayed for this—not sameness, but perfected unity: "that they may all be one; even as you, Father, are in me, and I in you..." (John 17:20–23).

This is the difference between biblical unity and New Age oneness. New Age thought collapses the self into sameness; the Holy Spirit reveals how every story matters. Your voice carries weight, your presence is needed, and your transformation contributes to the flourishing of the whole.

The Righteous Court

Jesus' descent was not because He needed purification—He was sinless. It was because we did. As Paul writes, "For him who knew no sin he made to be sin on our behalf, so that in him we might become the righteousness of God" (2 Corinthians 5:21). He became sin, but He did not stay sin. He carried the full weight of our chains—every curse, every accusation, every ordinance against us—into death itself and left them there. When He rose, He rose not clothed in sin, but clothed in glory—our shame exchanged for His righteousness, our death exchanged for His life. And because He was truly innocent, heaven's court could not condemn Him: "Which of you convicts me of sin?" (John 8:46); "who did no sin" (1 Peter 2:22); "tempted in all ways like we are, yet without sin" (Hebrews 4:15). The spotless Lamb could bear our guilt precisely because He had none of His own.

1. The Court of Heaven

In biblical imagery, heaven is a courtroom: "The judgment was set, and the books were opened" (Daniel 7:10). Satan is called "the accuser of our brothers" (Revelation 12:10), meaning he brings legal charges against us in God's court. When Adam sinned, he legally handed over dominion—so Satan could claim the right to enslave humanity.

2. How Jesus Overcame It

On the Cross, Jesus satisfied the demands of the court. "The wages of sin is death" (Romans 6:23), so He paid that wage on our behalf. Being sinless, He could be our substitute; in heaven's court, an innocent Man cannot be condemned. By becoming sin and dying in our place, He fulfilled the judgment and canceled the record against us: "He wiped out the handwriting of ordinances which was against us... having stripped the principalities and the powers, he made a show of them openly, triumphing over them in it" (Colossians

2:14–15). That's why He had to descend. He took our guilt and chains into death itself and left them there.

3. Our Part: Remaining in Him

The victory is real, but it becomes ours only when we are in Christ. "There is therefore now no condemnation to those who are in Christ Jesus" (Romans 8:1). Renewal is ongoing: "Be transformed by the renewing of your mind" (Romans 12:2). Why? Because if we agree with the enemy's lies, we give him a foothold (Ephesians 4:27).

4. The Foothold of Agreement

Agreement is never neutral. Adam's agreement enslaved humanity; our daily agreement with God or with the enemy determines what operates in our lives. Since the Cross, Satan has no true authority—only what we yield to him through lies, fear, or disobedience. This is why Scripture calls us to "take every thought captive to the obedience of Christ" (2 Corinthians 10:5).

Jesus overcame legally in the court of heaven. Practically, we must remain in Him, continually renewing our minds, or else Satan exploits old agreements and lies to gain access. Christ won the victory once for all; we walk it out daily by aligning with His truth through the Holy Spirit.

And yet, the path is not easy. The Holy Spirit still leads us into descent—the honest confrontation with wounds, patterns, and shadows—so that the fragments of light within us can be gathered and made whole again. Carl Jung described this as a descent into the underworld of the self, where the shadow must be faced. But for Christians, this is not only symbolic; it is lived reality. In Christ, the scattered pieces are gathered, the shadows healed, and the light restored. Many members, one body—united in the Spirit of truth.

And this is the language of the Bride. The many become one body in Christ, not through the erasure of individuality but through union in love. Just as Eve was drawn from the side of Adam, so the Church was born from the pierced side of Christ (John 19:34). At the Cross, He was not only redeeming individuals—He was gathering a Bride, bone of His bone and flesh of His flesh, formed from His sacrifice and made alive by His Spirit.

In that vision of humanity stepping into Him, I saw more than suffering—I saw covenant. The many becoming one in Him. The Cross was not only an altar of death but a marriage covenant sealed in blood, binding us forever to the Bridegroom.

Discernment in a World of False Light

Our pain and our blockages—those old memories, patterns, and lies—don't surface randomly. The Holy Spirit draws them out so that we can finally give them a voice. He whispers, "Yes, I saw what happened. You don't have to bury it anymore. Let's release it together." This is not punishment; it is preparation. Just as Jesus' descent ended in resurrection and ascension, our descent is not the end of the story. It is the very thing that prepares us to rise.

I saw this play out when I was raising my niece at age ten. She had already carried more pain than any child should. One day, I learned a friend had taught her about cutting. My heart sank, but I knew we had to face it. I told her, "Pain doesn't come out by creating more pain. It comes out when you give it a voice." She didn't need to bury her suffering deeper; she needed to bring it into the light where it could be acknowledged, carried, and transformed.

Just as my niece needed space to voice her pain, we too are invited by the Holy Spirit to bring our struggles into the light. The healing that followed in her life was gradual—there were setbacks and tears, but she learned that she was not alone. Over time, she became more willing to talk about her feelings, and I saw her reclaim a sense of hope. This experience shaped my own spiritual journey as well, teaching me the courage to face my own wounds and trust the Holy Spirit's guidance.

This is what the ascension process really looks like. It isn't about escaping hardship, but moving through it with faith—trusting that every challenge is part of a larger journey toward healing and growth. Similarly, "descent" refers to those times when the Holy Spirit leads us to face our inner shadows. It is never for punishment, but for transformation. In those moments, the Holy Spirit reminds us that we are being prepared for resurrection—just as Christ's descent into death led to new life for all.

He helps us discern where we are on the journey: "I'm in the wilderness right now," or "This feels like the death-before-resurrection part." And in those moments, He reminds us that God never sends us into chaos alone. "Yahweh himself, he it is who goes before you. He will be with you. He will not fail you nor forsake you. Don't be afraid. Don't be discouraged" (Deuteronomy 31:8).

That is the difference between wandering through a life without faith and walking with the Holy Spirit. He gives us enough light for the next step, enough confirmation to keep trusting: "I will instruct you and teach you in the way which you shall go. I will counsel you with my eye on you" (Psalm 32:8). The path of descent always carries the promise of ascent—for the cross is never the end, but the doorway to resurrection.

The New Creation

All of this—the stripping, the symptoms, the trials, the signs—points to one end: transformation.

"Therefore if anyone is in Christ, he is a new creation. The old things have passed away. Behold, all things have become new" (2 Corinthians 5:17).

Jesus' hero's journey is not distant history. It is the pattern written into our lives. The wilderness, the tests, the descent, even the strange symptoms of transformation—all of it is preparation.

The Holy Spirit doesn't erase identity. He refines it. He doesn't strip us for destruction but for resurrection. His goal is not to make us escape the world, but to embody heaven within it—to become living vessels of Christ's presence.

This is what it means to manifest with the Holy Spirit: not chasing blessings or signs, but allowing Christ's journey to be written into our own until we too are made new.

Chapter Six

Hidden Light and the Completion of the Pattern

This chapter is a little different from the others. Here, I share a collection of ideas—some drawn from science, some from mysticism, some from other writers, and some from my own reflections. A few of these are highly speculative, and I wrestled with whether to include them at all. After all, these are not pillars of the Christian faith, nor are they essential for salvation.

And yet, I chose to keep them because the heart of this book is about manifesting with the Holy Spirit—and that requires imagination. Too often, our subconscious is shaped by limiting beliefs, stories, and fears that keep us from seeing the fullness of what God longs to reveal. Sometimes the way to break free is to entertain ideas that stretch us, to explore metaphors that challenge old patterns, and to let wonder open new doors of faith.

At the same time, referring back to one of my favorite verses, Scripture exhorts us to "test all things; hold firmly that which is good" (1 Thessalonians 5:21). Every idea here, no matter how fascinating, must be tested against the guidance of the Holy Spirit. That's part of what I call my Ascension Bootcamp with Him: learning not to run from fears or unfamiliar ideas, but to bring them before God, to face them honestly, and to let the Holy Spirit sort truth from deception.

Too often, we separate church from "state," as though faith cannot speak to science, culture, or current events. But I believe it is vital for Christians to know what ideas are shaping our world—and even more vital to learn how to discern them through the Holy Spirit's wisdom.

If nothing else, I ask you to read this chapter as an allegory. Whether or not you agree with every hypothesis presented, let it serve as a reminder: God has hidden light within creation and within us, and the Holy Spirit awakens that light so we can live as vessels of heaven on earth. That is the point. The rest is scaffolding for the imagination—a way to picture what it means to rise, to be transformed, and to see the world through the lens of resurrection.

The Tomb as Womb and Abyss

Imagine standing outside that stone tomb. To the world, it looked like the end—sealed, dark, silent. Yet in God's design, it was not only a grave but also a womb. Before life burst forth, the tomb was also the inmost cave—the abyss at the heart of the Hero's Journey.

Every hero must face such a place: the darkest depths, the silence where hope seems swallowed, the stripping away of everything familiar. Campbell called this stage the inmost cave, where the hero confronts death itself—whether literal or symbolic.

Jesus entered this cave not as myth but as reality. His body lay in the abyss of death, His spirit descending into the depths, His disciples scattered in despair. And yet, He did not enter as one defeated but as One who would transform the cave itself. What looked like finality became threshold. The grave became a womb, birthing resurrection life and opening a new creation.

This is the pattern of the inmost cave: what seems like an ending becomes the place of transformation. And this rhythm of hiddenness is written everywhere in creation. Lightning splits the sky, rivers branch into deltas, trees spread their limbs, and even your lungs form tiny bronchioles. Fractals repeat endlessly, revealing God's fingerprints at every scale. The same divine design spirals through seashells and galaxies, echoing all the way into the hidden chambers of your own heart. Jesus said it plainly: "The Kingdom of God is within you" Luke 17:21. The hidden chambers of the world mirror the hidden chambers inside us—waiting for revelation.

Even your body carries this mystery. In the saddle-shaped hollow of the skull, the sella turcica cradles the pituitary gland, often called the master regulator of life-sustaining hormones. Nearby rests the pineal gland, attuned to light and rhythm, governing the circadian cycles of sleep and wakefulness. For centuries, mystics and philosophers have seen these two as spiritually significant. René Descartes called the pineal the "seat of the soul," while Eastern traditions associated it with the "third eye."

In the context of spirituality and manifesting, their symbolism becomes striking. The pineal connects us to light and rhythm, aligning our inner sense of time with creation. The pituitary governs growth and fruitfulness, images that

Scripture often uses to describe spiritual flourishing. It is as though God designed these hidden glands to echo His greater pattern: light guiding life, rhythm shaping growth, hidden chambers sustaining what is seen.

The pituitary, influencing growth, creativity, and desire, has often been viewed as the "master gland." Together they sit like twin lamps in the hidden chamber of the skull, quietly regulating both biological and perceptual life—echoes of the same design that turns graves into wombs, caves into thresholds, and endings into beginnings.

The tomb, then, is both abyss and womb. The mind, too, becomes a cave of encounter, where imagination and prayer open into communion with God. And the heart—with its quiet electromagnetic song, sixty times stronger than the brain's field—may well be the true inner sanctuary where the Holy Spirit writes eternity. Perhaps you've felt it: peace, joy, or love so profound it could only be the Holy Spirit tuning your heart to the melody of resurrection.

Other traditions have also recognized the significance of inner spaces. Hindu mysticism speaks of the Cave of Brahman—a hidden chamber of the heart where the seeker encounters ultimate reality. In that cave, silence gives way to illumination, and the soul is reborn into awareness. But here lies the difference: in Hindu thought, the cave points inward toward dissolution into the impersonal Absolute. In Christianity, the tomb is both inner and outer, both symbolic and historical. It is not only metaphor but event—the place where God acted in time and space to remake creation. Where the Cave of Brahman whispers of stillness, Christ's tomb bursts outward, shaking the earth, splitting history in two, and opening a future no human mind could have conceived.

Science, too, points us back to the heart. More than a pump, it has its own "mini-brain," an intricate network of nerves that communicates with the whole body. Its electromagnetic field can be detected several feet away, and when we experience love, gratitude, or peace, that field becomes beautifully coherent—as if the heart itself were singing in harmony with creation. No wonder Scripture emphasizes the heart as the seat of belief: "If you confess with your mouth that Jesus is Lord, and believe in your heart that God raised him from the dead, you will be saved." Jesus promised that He and the Father would make their home with those who love Him, and He made it simple: "How much more will your heavenly Father give the Holy Spirit to those who ask him?"

The Shroud and the Burst of Light

Picture the tomb again: darkness, silence, stone. To the watching world, it looked like the end. But then—an eruption of light. Was this not like the first moment of creation?

Light appears everywhere as a bridge. Biophotons flicker inside your cells, guiding growth and healing. Some researchers suggest the brain itself may use photons to communicate, meaning thought could literally be woven with light. In physics, light is the constant that shapes space and time, while quantum theory shows that observation collapses waves of light into measurable form. At every level, light connects matter, life, and awareness.

The Shroud of Turin deepens this mystery. Researchers studying the cloth have concluded that only an intense burst of radiation could have seared the image into the linen. The energy required would have been so great it could have blinded anyone nearby—even if the event took place in a sealed tomb. Whatever its cause, the shroud suggests the resurrection released a burst unlike anything ever measured on earth.

Here is the puzzle: if the resurrection released such unimaginable light, why was no one outside the tomb blinded by it? Was it God's hidden light—shielded from human eyes, yet powerful enough to alter the fabric of reality itself? Or could it be that those alive at the time were immersed in that same light, created within it even as Jesus was raised? Perhaps this was not only the dawn of new creation, but the very moment of creation itself—the same burst of energy scientists call the Big Bang.

What if the old testament, such as Genesis is not simply a sequential record but the backstory—like when a writer begins with the climax and then fills in the history that leads to it? In that sense, the resurrection may be the true central event, the wormhole through which all of time and creation flows. It is the axis where eternity touches history, establishing a kind of divine homeostasis that keeps reality itself in balance.

From eternity's perspective, where past and future fold into one, the burst of light that ignited the universe and the burst of light that poured from the empty tomb may be one continuous ripple of divine power. Scripture calls Jesus both the first Adam and the second Adam (1 Corinthians 15:45)—

the origin of humanity and its new beginning. He is also the Alpha and the Omega, the beginning and the end (Revelation 22:13). If He is both the starting point and the fulfillment, then the light of the resurrection may be the same hidden light that sparked creation itself. The Big Bang could have been the outward ripple of that eternal act, while the resurrection was its redemptive center—where history and eternity collided.

Fractals help us picture this mystery. The same pattern repeats at every scale: a seed dies in the soil before new life breaks through; a baby must leave the womb to be born; a dragonfly larva leaves the water to take flight in the air. Death to one environment becomes birth into another. The tomb follows this same pattern: both an ending and a beginning, a place of silence that erupts into life. What happens in seeds, wombs, and cocoons may be small reflections of what happened on the largest scale—the death and resurrection of Christ reverberating outward as the very structure of the cosmos.

Even our calendar bears witness. For centuries, time itself has been divided by Christ's life: B.C. (Before Christ) and A.D. (Anno Domini, "in the year of our Lord"). Modern culture may prefer B.C.E. and C.E., but the dividing line remains the same: history pivots on Christ's coming. Time itself acknowledges Him as the hinge of history—the axis where eternity intersects creation.

Scripture says, "Jesus Christ is the same yesterday, today, and forever" (Hebrews 13:8). If He is the axis of time, then the burst of resurrection light may reverberate both backward and forward through history, touching even the origin of the cosmos.

Jesus' ministry foreshadowed this union of light and life. When He raised Jairus' daughter, He said, "Talitha koum!" (Little girl, I say to you, arise) (Mark 5:41). The word for "arise" is the same later used for His own resurrection. With Lazarus, He declared, "I am the light of the world. Whoever follows me will not walk in the darkness, but will have the light of life" (John 8:12), then called into the tomb: "Lazarus, come out!" (John 11:43). Again and again, the pattern holds—where Jesus brings life, He brings light.

Paul writes, "For in him all things were created, in the heavens and on the earth, things visible and things invisible… all things have been created through him and for him. He is before all things, and in him all things hold together" (Colossians 1:16-17). The resurrection is not simply one event among many—it is the sustaining pulse of creation itself, the moment through which all life, past and future, is upheld in Christ.

And here we see the mystery of the hidden light of Genesis 1. Before the sun, moon, or stars were made, God said, "Let there be light" (Genesis 1:3). Jewish mystics called this the Or HaGanuz—the light hidden away after the fall, reserved for the righteous and for the age to come. What if the resurrection was the unveiling of that hidden light? The same radiance that birthed the cosmos, now breaking out of the tomb to ignite new creation.

If all creation came through Him, then it makes sense that eternal life can only be sustained in Him. To believe in Christ is to remain connected to the very Source of existence—the One in whom life began and the One in whom it continues forever. As Jesus said, "I am the way, the truth, and the life. No one comes to the Father except through me" (John 14:6).

This is why manifesting with the Holy Spirit is not about chasing vague energy or the illusions of New Age "light." It is about awakening to the divine light God planted within you—the hidden spark of His creation—now revealed through Christ. The Holy Spirit fans that spark into flame, aligning your heart with heaven's light so you can live as a vessel of resurrection power, bringing heaven to earth in your daily life.

So whether we see the resurrection and the Big Bang as symbolic echoes or literal convergences, the truth remains: life bursts forth from hiddenness, creation reignites in a flash, and as John testifies, "the light shines in the darkness, and the darkness hasn't overcome it" (John 1:5). The resurrection is not only the axis of faith—it may be, in ways beyond comprehension, the axis of the cosmos itself.

Resurrection and the Cosmos

Modern cosmology adds another layer of wonder to our search for meaning. In the early 20th century, Einstein's theory of general relativity revealed that space and time are not fixed backdrops but flexible fabrics, bending and curving under the influence of mass and energy. Decades later, the Planck spacecraft mapped the faint afterglow of the Big Bang—the Cosmic Microwave Background—and discovered subtle fluctuations larger than scientists expected. With 99%

certainty, the findings suggest that the universe may not be flat, but "closed."

Picture the universe not as an endless plane, but as a great sphere curving back on itself. In such a design, if you traveled far enough in one direction, you would eventually return to your starting point. Light itself would bend and loop, always returning to its source.

If creation is circular, then perhaps spiritual reality mirrors the same pattern. The planets, stars, and galaxies already move in circular rhythms. Through the holographic principle, physicists suggest that reality itself may be a projection, repeating at every scale. If creation is patterned this way, then it is reasonable to imagine that time itself could also be circular in nature. Scripture seems to echo this intuition: "For everything there is a season, and a time for every purpose under heaven" (Ecclesiastes 3:1). Life unfolds in cycles, not straight lines.

This further supports my hypothesis that the resurrection, then, may not simply be a moment in history—it may be the very center of the circle, the hinge on which all of history swings. The burst of divine light at the empty tomb could be the same event cosmologists glimpse in the Big Bang, reverberating backward and forward through curved spacetime.

Myths and Shadows Pointing to Christ

Even humanity's oldest stories faintly echo this rhythm. Osiris rising in Egypt, Persephone returning from the underworld in Greece—myths of death and rebirth etched into culture after culture. Campbell named this the Hero's Journey: the cycle of descent, ordeal, transformation, and return. Jung described it as the archetypal pattern of the collective unconscious, surfacing in every culture because it mirrors something buried deep in the human soul.

But Christianity proclaims something more. These stories are not equal to the Gospel; they are shadows pointing toward the real. As C.S. Lewis said, Christianity is the "myth become fact." The reason death-and-resurrection stories exist everywhere is because they are fractured beams of a greater light—rays refracted from the one true story that gives meaning to them all: the life, death, and resurrection of Jesus Christ.

And this story is not linear, but circular. In mathematics, the circle is the most perfect form: infinite, closed, every point equidistant from the center. In geometry, it represents wholeness. In physics, the very cosmos is built on circles and spirals. The earth rotates on its axis and orbits the sun. The sun itself, with our entire solar system, revolves around the center of the Milky Way galaxy. And the galaxies swirl in spirals, each one echoing the same design. The universe itself is written in orbits and returns.

Jesus' journey follows this same circle of light. He receives the call at the Jordan, where heaven opened and light descended. He descends into the wilderness, confronting the shadows. He surrenders in Gethsemane and sacrifices Himself on the Cross, when darkness covered the land. Then, at the tomb, the circle closed and opened at once: the abyss became a womb, death became birth, and hidden light erupted into new creation. From there the circle widened, as He returned with the Elixir—the Holy Spirit—poured out as fire and light upon His people.

The Hero's Journey is not just about storytelling—it is a fractal of the greater reality. Every myth, every parable, every narrative of descent and renewal is a shard of divine light scattered into human imagination. And just as planets circle stars, and stars circle galaxies, all these stories arc back to Christ. He is the axis at the center of the circle, the One in whom all scattered rays are gathered.

The Circle of Time

What if we take one more step of faith and ask: could the very nature of God reflect this cyclical reality? We confess one God who exists in three persons—Father, Son, and Holy Spirit—a divine circle of love encircling three distinct persons.

The Trinity has often been depicted as a triangle: three points connected by three sides. In geometry, the triangle is the most stable shape. It conveys strength, balance, and permanence—an image of God's unshakable nature. Yet a triangle also has fixed sides and sharp edges. It can unintentionally suggest hierarchy, as though one point sits above the others.

A circle tells a different story. A circle has no beginning and no end. Every point along its edge is equidistant from the center. It represents motion, eternity, and wholeness. In this light, the Trinity is less like a static triangle of lines and more like a living circle of eternal exchange. The Father pours love into the Son, the Son returns love to the Father, and the Holy Spirit proceeds as the bond of that love, completing the circle. Unlike a triangle that suggests order by separation, the circle reveals order by flow—a ceaseless rhythm of divine life, without division, without end.

Science, too, points us back to the circle. String theory proposes that at the smallest scale of reality, matter is not made of particles but of tiny vibrating strings of energy. And most of these strings are not straight—they are loops. Their endless circular vibrations determine whether they manifest as light, matter, or force. The circle, then, is not just a metaphor for divine life but may be the literal foundation of the universe.

What string theory describes—the universe held together by tiny vibrating loops—echoes the Trinity's eternal circulation of love. At both the cosmic and the quantum level, creation is upheld not by rigid edges but by living cycles. Hidden dimensions of reality may even be curled into circular forms too small to see, reminding us of the hidden light of creation and the concealed chambers where God works unseen until revelation bursts forth.

From the smallest vibrating string to the orbit of Earth around the sun, from the spiral arms of galaxies to the eternal circle of Father, Son, and Holy Spirit, creation repeats this geometry of wholeness. The circle is not just a shape—it is the rhythm of divine order, a fractal signature of the God who is love.

Plus, creation further reflects this pattern. Through fractals and the holographic principle, we see reality repeating at every scale. Cells mirror the structure of organs, which mirror the design of the body, which mirrors the patterns of nations, ecosystems, galaxies, and even the cosmos itself. Seasons turn in cycles of death and rebirth, echoing the same rhythm of descent and resurrection.

Even myth intuited this: Hindu mysticism describes gods creating and destroying worlds in endless cycles, sensing something of the eternal rhythm. And yet Christianity reveals the fullness: life infinitely expresses God in ways that reflect His own eternal mystery. Time itself, like creation, may not be a line with a beginning and end, but a circle curved around God's eternal still point.

Step back and see the whole: at the center is the Father, "For in him we live, move, and have our being" (Acts 17:28). On the circumference stands Christ: His resurrection on one side, His return on the other. Christ is the Arc—the living curve bridging eternity and history, the visible sweep of God's eternal movement through time.

And you—your wilderness, your shadows, your hidden caves—are part of that circle. These are not detours but essential spirals, leading you again and again closer to the Center. The Holy Spirit walks with you, transforming every descent into resurrection, every shadow into light, every hiddenness into revelation.

In this way, science, myth, and Scripture converge: time is not linear but circular, curved around the eternal nature of God Himself. This is true ascension: Holy Spirit-led, God-centered, and overflowing with Christ's glory—until the circle finally closes in His return.

If you think about it, the Incarnation itself carries this cyclical mystery. God impregnated Mary with Himself—the

Father, through the Holy Spirit, conceiving the Son. He became both the Giver and the Gift, the Source and the Seed. The Creator entered creation, not as an outsider but as one of us, so that humanity could be restored to divinity through Him.

In this, we glimpse the same fractal pattern: God at the center, yet spiraling outward into the world He made, only to draw it back into Himself. The circle of Father, Son, and Holy Spirit widened to include us, so that what was lost in Adam could be regained in Christ.

The cycle of God's nature—eternal love flowing between Father, Son, and Holy Spirit—overflowed into time through Mary's womb, so that eternity itself could take on flesh. And in the resurrection, that cycle was completed: the Son returning to the Father, now carrying humanity with Him.

Rahab as Pattern

Have you ever wondered whether this is the first time heaven and earth have existed in this form? Scripture promises a day when Christ will return, and with Him, "a new heaven and a new earth" (Revelation 21:1). That alone suggests that creation is not fixed, but can be remade. And if it will be remade once, could it have been remade before?

Thinkers like Braden, Alberino, Robert Edward Grant, Dolores Cannon, and Alexander Quinn have all raised possibilities of multiple cycles of creation. Braden and Cannon imagine the earth as once envisioned as a kind of "school" or reward ground for higher-dimensional beings.

Alberino points to extraterrestrial encounters and ancient ruins as potential remnants of previous ages. Grant and Quinn lean into the mathematics of cycles, showing how history, numbers, and symbols repeat like clockwork.

When God first told me to write this book, I didn't know where to begin. I thought it might be my memoir, so I pulled out books on writing character arcs. If Jesus is the main character of history, as Alberino suggests, and I am only a supporting role, then I realized I needed to write a character bio for God Himself. That meant asking: what is His "why"? What motivates Him?

The Holy Spirit led me into the prophets, especially Jeremiah. There, I noticed God's language. He spoke of cities as unfaithful women, of idolatry as adultery, of covenant-breaking as sexual betrayal. It startled me at first—but slowly, I began to understand: to God, sin is not an abstract crime, but the breaking of intimate love. Idolatry wounds His heart as deeply as a spouse's betrayal.

This connects to the ancient puzzle of Rahab. In Joshua, Rahab is a prostitute whose faith saves her household. In Job and Psalms, Rahab is described as a cosmic monster, perhaps even a planet subdued by God's power. Alberino suggests that Rahab was a celestial body destroyed in judgment.

How can Rahab be a woman, a nation, and a planet? The answer is in the pattern: God often uses one name across multiple scales. Jacob becomes Israel, Israel becomes a nation. What begins as a person expands into a people, then a destiny. Rahab, in every form, represents chaos, rebellion, and pride—yet also redemption. She is a prostitute, yet saved by faith. She is a monster, yet subdued by God. She is Jericho's shame, yet a foremother of Christ. The pattern repeats: woman, city, nation, world.

And here we come to humanity's repeating sins. Over and over, God rebukes His people for two things: idolatry and sexual immorality. These are the fractal failures of humanity. Adam's sin was idolatry—trusting creation's voice over God's. Eve's role is debated. Scripture only says she knew Adam, but some traditions whisper that the serpent's deception was more intimate than we imagine. Whether literal or symbolic, the point remains: the enemy's scheme has always been to corrupt what God made pure, whether through false worship or false intimacy.

And if time is cyclical, if creation has unfolded in multiple rounds, then how many times has the enemy repeated these same deceptions? How many times has Satan tainted women, families, and nations? How many civilizations, now only ruins, collapsed under the weight of these sins? We cannot know the number. But the pattern is clear. Like a hologram repeating at every scale, the same brokenness emerges: idolatry and sexual immorality—the two fractures that wound covenantal love.

The Mystery of the Second Eve

If Jesus is the Second Adam, then the question naturally arises: who is the Second Eve? Scripture is clear that the Church is called the Bride of Christ, but the patterns of Scripture suggest that this image may also echo through individuals, nations, and archetypes.

Genesis tells us Eve was created as a "helper suitable" for Adam (Genesis 2:18). Yet the Hebrew phrase *ezer kenegdo* carries a depth far richer than our English translations often convey: it means a counterpart, a strength opposite him, almost like a mirror in which Adam could see himself completed. Some Jewish mystics take this to suggest that Adam's true "bride" was never Eve alone, but Israel itself—the people of God called into covenant (Which sounds an awful lot like Jesus). In this view, Eve's role was archetypal, representing humanity in its vulnerability to deception, but also in its capacity for restoration.

Others read Eve as the first archetype of the Bride of Christ. She was drawn from Adam's side while he slept, just as the Church was drawn from the pierced side of the Second Adam, Christ, when blood and water flowed at His death (John 19:34). In this light, Eve's union with Adam was not the ultimate marriage but a shadow pointing forward to the greater covenant of Christ and His Bride.

Through the fractal lens, Eve is more than one woman. She is a pattern: the first "city," the first "nation," the first "bride." Just as Rahab was both a woman and a city, and Jacob was both a man and a nation, Eve is both Adam's companion and a prophetic symbol of humanity's covenant with God.

Mary as Archetypes of the Bride

In the New Testament, many women named Mary appear, each reflecting facets of the redeemed feminine:

- **Mary, the mother of Jesus** represents faith, surrender, and the paradox of virginity and motherhood. She is the New Eve in one sense, for where Eve grasped, Mary received.

- **Mary Magdalene** embodies devotion and witness. She was the first to proclaim the risen Christ, a mark of profound intimacy—but not of earthly marriage. One common tactic of the accuser is to undermine Christ's sinlessness by proposing a romantic tie between Jesus and Mary Magdalene. If such a claim were true, it would either entail sexual sin or a knowingly breaking covenant to leave behind a widow, both of which would violate holiness and disqualify Him as the spotless Lamb. But Scripture's witness is consistent: "in him is no sin" (1 John 3:5); He challenges, "Which of you convicts me of sin?" (John 8:46). These rumors function to attack the legal foundation of our salvation; they do not stand in the light of the Gospel. And goes to demonstrate those that supposedly channel Mary Magdelene are dealing with a deceiving spirit. Jesus abstained from wedlock, for His covenant was greater than one household; His Bride was cosmic and eternal. Their friendship reminds us of what redeemed intimacy can look like between man and woman: pure, faithful, devoted without corruption.
- **Mary of Bethany** points to worship, sitting at Jesus' feet and anointing Him for burial. She reflects the Bride's longing for communion and costly love.

Together, these Marys form a composite image of the Bride. Each Mary, in her own way, mirrors Eve but also foreshadows the Second Eve—the true Bride awaiting her union with Christ.

Israel, the Church, and the New Jerusalem

In the prophets, Israel is often personified as God's unfaithful bride—a nation portrayed as a woman who strays after idols. Yet even in her unfaithfulness, God promises restoration: "I will betroth you to me forever" (Hosea 2:19).

The New Testament carries this imagery forward: the Church is purified as the Bride of Christ (Ephesians 5:25-27), and Revelation culminates with the New Jerusalem descending from heaven "prepared like a bride adorned for her husband" (Revelation 21:2). Thus the Bride is simultaneously a people, a city, and a cosmic reality.

The Second Eve Yet to Come

But what if, in keeping with Scripture's fractal patterns, the Bride is not only collective and cosmic, but also singular? Just as Jacob became Israel and Israel became a nation, just as Rahab was a woman, a city, and perhaps even a planet, the Bride could appear at multiple scales: the Church, the New Jerusalem, and perhaps also a singular woman.

Christian tradition has seen Mary, the mother of Jesus, as the New Eve in one sense, because she reversed Eve's disobedience by her faithful "yes." But others, like Palvanov and strands of Jewish mysticism, have speculated that the messianic age may include a feminine counterpart to restore cosmic balance. While Christianity does not teach that another messiah will come, the idea points toward a truth Scripture confirms: the story is incomplete until Bride and Bridegroom are united.

Thus, the Second Eve may not be one woman only, but a layered archetype:

- In **Mary**, we see Eve redeemed.
- In **the Church**, we see the Bride made ready.
- In **New Jerusalem**, we see creation itself adorned.
- And at the consummation of all things, there may yet be a singular feminine figure who embodies the Bride in personal form, standing beside Christ, the Second Adam, when heaven and earth are made new.

Eve began as mother of the living, but her story fractured into sin. Mary bore the Life of the world, but pointed beyond herself to the greater Bride. The Church carries the covenant in history, and New Jerusalem will carry it in eternity. The Second Eve, however she is revealed, will embody the union of all these layers: humanity restored, creation redeemed, covenant completed.

The Completion of the Pattern

I believe this matters now more than ever, because we are living near the end of days. Revelation's vision of the Bride is not abstract; it is a summons to readiness. And yet, the Church today is not ready for His return. Surveys consistently show a steep decline in practicing Christians: fewer believers pray daily, fewer read Scripture regularly, and many churches are dwindling. The Bride, it seems, is drowsy rather than awake.

Jesus Himself warned of this in the parable of the ten virgins (Matthew 25:1–13). Five were wise, keeping their lamps filled with oil, while five were foolish, unprepared when the Bridegroom arrived. The oil represents the Holy Spirit—the hidden light within us that must be kept burning. Without Him, the Bride is not ready. With Him, she shines at the midnight hour.

And here the Hero's Journey circles to its close. After the descent into death and the triumph of resurrection, the Hero returns with the Elixir—the gift that transforms the community. For Jesus, that Elixir is the Holy Spirit. He is the treasure brought back from the abyss, the oil for our lamps, the hidden light that makes the Bride ready. This is why teaching people to manifest with the Holy Spirit is so urgent. Manifesting in this sense is Holy Spirit-led preparation: learning to live as vessels of the hidden light, embodying heaven on earth now.

The Second Eve is not only a prophetic archetype of the future—she is already being formed in us. Holy Spirit-led. Christ-centered. Radiant with the hidden light of new creation. Ready to meet the Bridegroom when He comes.

Chapter Seven

The Nature of Emotion

When I first began exploring the connection between thought, imagination, and manifestation, I understood the power of belief and the spoken word. But one question still troubled me: what about emotion? If the goal of spirituality was to remain calm, collected, and detached, why would God create us with such a wide spectrum of feelings?

It was only later, through prayer and study, that I began to see emotions not as distractions to be controlled, but as frequencies of the soul. Negative emotions like anger, grief, and fear are heavy, dense, and grounding. Positive emotions like joy, gratitude, and love are light, expansive, and uplifting. Both serve a purpose: negative emotion grounds and transmutes trauma and sin, while positive emotion raises us closer to God's frequency, pressing into the very fabric of our DNA.

Elements: Creation's Mirror

The Gospel of the Essenes—though not part of Scripture—still lead me to an interesting concept. It portrays Jesus as teaching about the four angels of Air, Water, Fire, and Earth, each representing a force of creation and renewal. Air refreshes and gives breath, water cleanses and nourishes, fire purifies and transforms, and earth grounds and sustains.

When viewed this way, our emotions mirror these elements: the breath that steadies us, the tears that cleanse us, the fire of passion that transforms us, and the grounding heaviness that draws us back to stability.

- **Air** reminds us of the Holy Spirit who moves like the wind: "The wind blows where it wants to, and you hear its sound, but don't know where it comes from and where it is going. So is everyone who is born of the Spirit" (John 3:8).
- **Water** recalls Jesus' promise: "But whoever drinks of the water that I will give him will never thirst again; but the water that I will give him will become in him a well of water springing up to eternal life" (John 4:14).
- **Fire** echoes Pentecost: "Tongues like fire appeared and were distributed to them, and one sat on each of them" (Acts 2:3). And it also reminds us of Daniel's words: "Many shall be purified, made white, and refined; but the wicked shall do wickedly" (Daniel 12:10). Fire doesn't only destroy—it refines.
- **Earth** points us back to our origin: "Yahweh God formed man from the dust of the ground, and breathed into his nostrils the breath of life; and man became a living soul" (Genesis 2:7). The earth still testifies to this truth. Just as dirt comes in shades of red, brown, black, yellow, and white across the globe, so too does human skin—each tone reflecting the colors of the soil from which God shaped us.

Together, these remind us that emotion is not accidental—it is elemental. God designed our inner life to work with creation's rhythms, not against them.

The Essene letters also portray Jesus as speaking of Earth as our mother. This made me pause. Could the Fourth Commandment, "Honor your father and your mother, that your days may be long in the land which Yahweh your God gives you" (Exodus 20:12), extend beyond biological parents to mean God the Father and Earth the Mother? Is this another multidimensional metaphor similar to that of Israel and Rahab?

I had to look them up on my phone to make sure I was seeing this correctly. The first three commandments honor God, and the last six deal with sins, yet the fourth seems to stand at a threshold. "Honor your father and your mother, as Yahweh your God commanded you, that your days may be long and that it may go well with you in the land which Yahweh your God gives you" (Deuteronomy 5:16). Understood in this new way, it becomes less awkward and more profound: to honor both heaven and earth is to remain balanced in body and spirit, rooted yet ascending.

This balance reminds me of the Tree of Life. Its roots sink deep into the soil, drawing strength and nourishment from the earth, while its branches stretch upward toward heaven, receiving light and life from above. In the same way, we are called to be both grounded and lifted—anchored in creation yet continually reaching for the Creator. As Proverbs says, "She is a tree of life to those who lay hold of her. Happy is everyone who retains her" (Proverbs 3:18).

Earth's Heartbeat and Human Resonance

Modern science has discovered that the Earth itself has a rhythm. The Schumann Resonances are a set of frequencies produced by electromagnetic waves trapped in Earth's lower ionosphere, ranging from the fundamental 7.83 Hz—often called the Earth's "heartbeat"—up to 33.8 Hz. These frequencies are generated primarily through global lightning activity, but they are also shaped by the Earth's magnetic field.

Here the geodynamo theory comes into play. Scientists believe Earth's magnetic field is generated by the motion of molten iron in its outer core, creating electric currents that sustain a protective shield around the planet. This shield not only protects us from harmful solar radiation but also influences the frequencies of the Schumann Resonances. Just as the sun is currently undergoing a magnetic pole flip, evidence suggests Earth's poles are slowly shifting as well—a reminder that our planet is dynamic, alive, and constantly in motion.

This heartbeat of the Earth interacts with our own rhythms. Studies have shown that human brainwaves, particularly in meditative or restful states, can synchronize with the Schumann frequencies. It is as if our bodies are designed to resonate with the planet itself, a reminder of Genesis 2:7: "Yahweh God formed man from the dust of the ground, and breathed into his nostrils the breath of life; and man became a living soul."

In the same way, we also experience spiritual pole flips. These are the wilderness seasons of the Hero's Journey—

when God strips away what is familiar and forces us to rely on Him alone. Israel wandered forty years in the desert before entering the Promised Land, and in a comparable way, each believer faces deserts of testing before breakthroughs of promise.

Hezekiah's Sign and the Shift of Frequencies

Hezekiah himself lived through such a reversal. When the prophet Isaiah told him to set his house in order because he would die, Hezekiah turned his face to the wall and wept bitterly before the Lord. His emotions surged like a storm, yet instead of being drowned in despair, he grounded himself in prayer. God responded, extending his life by fifteen years and granting him a sign in the heavens—the shadow on the sundial moving backward (Isaiah 38:5-8). This was more than a physical healing; it was a shift in frequency, a movement from the low resonance of death and despair into the higher resonance of promise and renewed authority.

Like Hezekiah, we too encounter these emotional storms when the frequencies around us seem destabilized. They mirror the solar storms in creation, where gamma rays and magnetic reversals shake the heavens and even move the earth's crust, triggering earthquakes, volcanic eruptions, and tsunamis. In the spirit, these storms shake us internally—our appetites, our emotions, our attachments—testing whether we will cling to old densities or rise into the higher vibration of trust. Hezekiah's breakthrough reminds us that God does not set us up to fail. The Promised Land cannot be entered in our old frequency, weighed down by fear, sin, and spiritual blindness.

This is why the wilderness is not punishment, but preparation. Kabbalistic tradition suggests that in the world to come, humanity will rule over planets. Whether literal or symbolic, the point aligns with modern science's vision of fractals and the holographic principle: our bodies are microcosms of galaxies. Each cell is like a star, each organ a solar system, together forming a cosmos of flesh and spirit. If we cannot steward our inner universe—our thoughts, our emotions, even our food choices—how can we expect to steward creation? As Jesus said, "He who is faithful in a very little is faithful also in much" (Luke 16:10).

Appetite, Food, and Spiritual Authority

This is why the enemy attacks food, cravings, and appetite. Poisoned soil, pesticide-laden crops, hormone-altered meats, and even microplastics in water all distort the body's God-given design. Our diet not only affects physical health but emotional stability and spiritual perception. To master emotion is also to master appetite, because both are energy flowing through the body. When these streams are polluted, leadership collapses. But when they are purified through discipline and the Holy Spirit's power, the soul resonates with heaven's frequency—and the believer becomes the kind of leader God intended in His Kingdom.

From Eden's fruit, to Israel's grumbling for meat, to Jesus being tempted in the desert, food has always been the stage where idolatry shows itself. This is why fasting has always been a holy practice: it breaks the chains of dependency, teaches us mastery over cravings, and re-centers our hunger on God Himself. In manifesting with the Holy Spirit, fasting cuts ties to the idols of consumption and opens us to the lighter, cleaner food of heaven. As we ascend, we may even notice our appetites shifting. Heavier, denser foods lose their appeal, while lighter, life-giving foods feel more aligned with the Holy Spirit's movement within us. Scripture itself hints at this transformation, when it speaks of the coming age where "the wolf and the lamb will feed together" (Isaiah 65:25). The imagery suggests not only harmony in creation, but also a new way of being—one where survival no longer depends on devouring, but on peace.

Modern science even confirms that our emotions and mental health are shaped by forces beyond ourselves. The sun, for instance, constantly erupts with solar flares that disturb Earth's magnetic field, causing geomagnetic storms. These storms don't only affect satellites and power grids—they ripple into human biology, influencing sleep, mood, and emotional stability. The sun is even undergoing a magnetic pole reversal, a phenomenon accompanied by intensified solar activity. These cosmic storms reflect the inner storms we face, reminding us that creation itself testifies to the reality of spiritual warfare and transformation.

We cannot enter the Promised Land in our old frequencies. God leads us through wilderness seasons to refine us—body, soul, and spirit—until our density matches the higher resonance of His promises. Israel's cravings were tested in the desert. They longed for the meat of Egypt but were instead given manna—light, heavenly food. This was not punishment, but preparation. It was a recalibration of appetite, teaching them to receive sustenance from heaven rather than bondage.

Ascension Symptoms: What You Might Feel

For me it started—unexpectedly—with cussing. I couldn't figure out why until a Smith Wigglesworth audiobook surfaced in my Audible feed. He taught that the Holy Spirit often brings residue to the surface so it can be released and make room for God's abundance. Soon after, images in my mind's eye weren't "just imagination." The Holy Spirit told me I would begin seeing in the spirit. Walking my dogs one evening, I sensed angels in a field beside me—like a stadium cheering a milestone. Later came a whirling, swirling energy in my abdomen, bouts of lightheadedness, and (surprisingly) a lifted spirit—I showed up to work in a good mood. Months in, deeper emotions surfaced. Because of PTSD I'd learned to "switch off," so sudden tears over small things were really buried grief bubbling up. They never lasted more than a day—though some were geysers.

What it may feel like (examples).

- Appetite shifts; cravings quiet; desire for "lighter" foods; increased thirst.
- Detox sensations: edgy speech surfacing without anger; irritability or old habits rising to be released.
- Somatic shifts: swirling warmth in the abdomen/chest; lightheadedness; fatigue waves; sleep pattern changes; head pressure.

- Perceptual sensitivity: vivid inner imagery, symbolic dreams; sensing angelic help; heightened discernment.
- Emotional releases: brief crying spells, repentance/forgiveness bursts—followed by uplift and peace.

Scripture-anchored signs (how I experienced them).
- Waves of grief rising and releasing — "Those who sow in tears will reap in joy" (Psalm 126:5).
- Anxiety surfacing, then peace settling — "In nothing be anxious… and the peace of God… will guard your hearts and your thoughts in Christ Jesus" (Philippians 4:6–7).
- Old bitterness bubbling up before forgiveness flowed — "Let all bitterness, wrath, anger… be put away… and be kind to one another" (Ephesians 4:31–32).
- Restless nights and vivid dreams pointing deeper — "Your sons and your daughters will prophesy… your old men will dream dreams" (Acts 2:17).
- Sudden fatigue, as if God Himself were forcing rest — "Come to me, all you who labor and are heavily burdened, and I will give you rest" (Matthew 11:28).
- Bursts of joy and clarity — "God's Kingdom is… righteousness, peace, and joy in the Holy Spirit" (Romans 14:17).
- A burning in my heart when His truth broke through — "Wasn't our heart burning within us, while he spoke to us along the way…?" (Luke 24:32).

How to walk it out with the Holy Spirit.
- Fast simply; hydrate well; favor whole, uncomplicated foods.
- Pray Scripture aloud; renounce lies the Spirit surfaces and replace them with truth (2 Corinthians 10:5; John 8:32).
- Journal releases (what surfaced → what God spoke). Add gentle movement, worship, and quiet.
- Reduce overstimulating media; bless your home with prayer and Scripture.
- If old grief/PTSD rises, invite the Comforter and, when needed, a trauma-informed Christian counselor (2 Corinthians 1:3–4).
- Test impressions; keep what aligns with Scripture (1 Thessalonians 5:21; 1 John 4:1).

Always rule out medical causes first; use this as a reference after evaluation. I spent 2018–2021 chasing answers (EEG for seizures, migraine care, profound daytime sleepiness). Only later, after relocating, did I receive a rheumatoid arthritis diagnosis. In hindsight, some "energy" issues overlapped with grief and trauma physiology. Seek care promptly for red flags (new/severe chest pain, fainting, persistent neurologic deficits, suicidal thoughts, rapid weight loss, fevers, or anything that worries you). Wise medical care is often part of the Spirit's provision. The world might call these "ascension symptoms." Scripture calls them sanctification. The Holy Spirit draws buried pain and blockages to the surface to release them, replacing them with peace, joy, and fire. What looks like breakdown is often breakthrough.

Clearing the Old, Carrying the Glory

We don't "jump" into holiness overnight; we're changed in stages. Our bodies are temples (1 Corinthians 6:19) and need time to acclimate to the Holy Spirit's "voltage." Scripture names this slow, steady increase: we are transformed "from glory to glory" (2 Corinthians 3:18) and grow "from faith to faith" (Romans 1:17). That is why old energy and trauma must be cleared—through repentance, forgiveness, renouncing false agreements, and renewing the mind (Hebrews 12:1; 2 Corinthians 10:5; Romans 12:2). Fasting helps both body and soul make room: it lowers the noise of appetite so the nervous system, emotions, and attention can adjust to the Spirit's higher resonance.

In the same way, fasting and the reordering of our appetites are not random disciplines but sacred trainings. If we cling to lower densities—old cravings, destructive emotions, or unrenewed thought patterns—we fail to see with the Holy Spirit and stumble at the threshold of our inheritance. But when we allow the Spirit to raise us, to still the inner storms, and to shift our appetites, we enter a higher frequency that aligns with the very atmosphere of the Promised Land.

This is why not everyone will hear or receive the depths of this teaching. If one is not yet ready for their Hero's Journey season, much of what is spoken here may sound like riddles. Yet for those being drawn into deeper transformation, these truths are the very bread of preparation. As Paul wrote, "But the natural man doesn't receive the things of God's Spirit, for they are foolishness to him, and he can't know them, because they are spiritually discerned" (1 Corinthians 2:14).

This is also why God draws us into wilderness seasons of separation. Not everyone can walk with us on the path to our purpose. They have their own journeys to complete, and though their frequencies may harmonize with ours for a time, the alignment often shifts as God refines us. What once felt like companionship can become dissonance, not because of failure, but because the Holy Spirit is calling us to tune more closely to His voice. It is in this solitude that intimacy with God is forged.

Yet this intimacy often proves bittersweet. Many discover, after the refining work is done, that the cost of transformation is both the loss of old alignments and the gain of new authority. The wilderness, then, is not a delay but a divine setup. It is the proving ground where appetites are purified, emotions are tempered, and the soul is taught to ride the waves of inner weather with God's peace. And just as Hezekiah saw a sign in the sundial moving backward (Isaiah 38:8), so too God gives us signs in creation that mirror our inward transformation. Only then can one emerge not merely as a survivor, but as a leader—ready to steward the Promised Land with the clarity, compassion, and resonance of heaven itself.

Counterfeit 5D vs. True Ascension

New Age spirituality often speaks of "ascending to the fifth dimension," as if humanity were evolving into a higher dimension of light and love. The language sounds biblical—frequency shifts, awakenings, new realities—but it is a counterfeit gospel. In this framework, ascension is achieved by human effort, meditation, or energetic alignment, bypassing repentance and the cross. It promises godhood without God, power without purification, frequency without faith.

A reality check from creation itself: we are not sitting still. Our entire solar system orbits the Milky Way, and the universe itself is expanding as space stretches. There isn't a single privileged "center" of this expansion; from any vantage, distant galaxies recede. In other words, the cosmos is dynamic and God-governed—not a fixed ladder we climb by technique. We don't self-elevate to a new earth; we are raised by the Holy Spirit into the mind of Christ.

This isn't new: the historic Christian path. What the world now markets as "ascension symptoms" has long been recognized in the Church as the stages of sanctification—tested by Scripture and witnessed by saints. "Beloved, don't believe every spirit, but test the spirits..." (1 John 4:1).

- St. John of the Cross – Dark Night of the Soul. God lovingly withdraws false supports so the soul learns to rest on Him alone. What feels like loss is purification for deeper union; old attachments and illusions are stripped so love can be pure.

- St. Teresa of Ávila – The Interior Castle. The soul journeys room by room (mansions) toward the center where God dwells. Prayer, silence, and surrender move us inward; distractions fall off, affections are reordered, and intimacy grows.
- Evelyn Underhill – Fivefold rhythm. A common pattern appears in mature believers: awakening → purification → illumination → dark night of the soul → union. These "symptoms" are not cosmic novelties; they are the birth pangs of transformation as the Holy Spirit conforms us to Christ.

In short, these movements are not the result of channeling spirits or climbing vibrational ladders; they are the Holy Spirit's age-old work of making us holy—what Scripture calls being changed "from glory to glory" (2 Corinthians 3:18).

While 5D teachings speak of a "higher vibrational realm," the focus remains on the self. The work is not outward but inward, centering on personal vibration and identity rather than obedience and service. Lightworkers are told that their mere existence is "enough" to raise the earth's frequency. But in this worldview there are no good works of mercy, no deliverance for those still bound, no breaking of strongholds. Yet Scripture tells us plainly: "Even so faith, if it has no works, is dead in itself" (James 2:17). The true test of transformation is not vibration but fruit—whether lives are freed, healed, and reconciled to God.

This teaching also overlooks the reality of spiritual agreements—covenants people have unknowingly entered that give the enemy a foothold. Paul reminds us, "The weapons of our warfare are not of the flesh, but mighty before God to the throwing down of strongholds, throwing down imaginations and every high thing that is exalted against the knowledge of God, and bringing every thought into captivity to the obedience of Christ" (2 Corinthians 10:4–5). Light alone does not dismantle lies; only the authority of Christ breaks chains.

God's reality is different. The true ascension is not climbing into "5D consciousness," but being raised by the Holy Spirit into the mind of Christ. It is not about escaping the material world but redeeming it. Where New Age teachings tell you to "look within" for your higher self, the gospel calls us to die to self and be raised with Christ. Where 5D spirituality frames history as humanity evolving into divinity, Scripture reveals history as God restoring creation through His Son, with the final convergence coming not by human vibration but by the return of the King.

The wilderness seasons and Promised Land seasons make this difference plain. Israel could not enter Canaan until they had shed the appetites of Egypt, because the Promised Land operates on a different frequency—holiness, faith, and obedience. In the same way, we cannot enter our inheritance while clinging to the lower vibrations of sin, self-will, and idolatry. True ascension is not a consciousness upgrade; it is crucifixion of the flesh and resurrection life.

New Age thought notices that appetites and emotions carry "frequency," but it mistakes both source and solution. Yes, food, cravings, and toxins can distort the body's design. Yes, emotions ripple through us like waves. But discipline and detox alone cannot usher in the Kingdom. Without the Holy Spirit, such practices tend toward self-glorification or deeper deception. Fasting, by contrast, is God's appointed way to cut idolatry at the root. It shifts appetite from lower density to heavenly food, not by self-effort but by dependence on God.

Just as the shadow on Hezekiah's sundial reversed as a sign of God's promise (Isaiah 38:8), so history's shadow will bend at the end of the age. Time itself may feel circular to us—measured in cycles like the earth's yearly path around the sun—yet all of history is being drawn toward Christ. New Age 5D promises a higher realm of vibration, but it stops short—it reflects the self, not the Savior. The circular sundial reminds us that only God has authority over time, space, and destiny. What He turns back, no human frequency can alter; what He accelerates, no counterfeit ascension can duplicate.

"This is why Jesus said, 'Man shall not live by bread alone, but by every word that proceeds out of the mouth of God'" (Matthew 4:4). The Word is the true bread. The Holy Spirit is the true frequency. And when our appetites and emotions are aligned with Him, we step into the higher resonance of the Promised Land—not by self-ascension, but by divine invitation.

Chapter Eight

Renewal Lived Out in Practice

Up to this point, we've been immersed in a kind of mind-bath—washed in the Word, stretched by symbols, and invited to see time, energy, and even our own thoughts through a new lens. Renewal always begins in the mind, because the mind is the gate where thoughts, emotions, and frequencies either align with heaven or drift into distortion. But the renewed mind alone is not the finish line—it is the foundation.

Now comes the next step: learning how to live this renewal out in practice. Manifestation with the Holy Spirit isn't powered by intellect or imagination alone; it flows through daily choices, actions, and alignments. All the revelation, all the vision, all the imagination in the world remains potential until it is put into motion.

Obedience as Coachability

That's where obedience comes in. Obedience is the activation point—the switch that turns revelation into reality. It's what moves manifestation from concept to creation. Without obedience, we stay in theory; with obedience, the Holy Spirit brings fruit.

When people hear the word obedience, it often stirs something uncomfortable. It sounds rigid. Controlling. For some, it might even conjure images of religious abuse or authoritarian parenting. In a modern world that values independence and freedom of thought, obedience feels outdated at best—and at worst, oppressive.

But that's the problem: we tend to interpret God's ways through human definitions. God's version of obedience is nothing like the world's. It's not about control or domination—it's about being teachable. It's about becoming coachable.

God can't train a closed heart. He can't teach someone who isn't willing to receive instruction. He may offer love unconditionally, but growth requires participation. Obedience is what opens the door to that process. And when it's your time to learn it, you'll know. For me, the word obey began showing up everywhere—magazines, ads, sermons. I couldn't escape it.

So I asked, "Okay, Lord, what do I need to obey?"

Learning to Pray with the Spirit

The answer came in stages. I had to learn how to pray. Not just rote recitations like I was taught growing up Catholic, but real, living prayer. I had to learn how to praise. Not just songs on Sunday, but lifting my hands, my eyes, my whole being to heaven in both joy and celebration. And I had to learn how to repent. Not just confess to get relief—but to turn, really turn, and walk in a new direction.

Yes, God wants us to have a secret place for prayer, just like Jesus talked about in Matthew 6. Yes, He cares about our posture. If you are physically able, He wants you to kneel. Scripture shows this again and again: "Oh come, let's worship and bow down. Let's kneel before Yahweh, our Maker" (Psalm 95:6). He invites us to lift our hands in surrender: "Lift up your hands in the sanctuary. Bless Yahweh!" (Psalm 134:2). Even bowing the head and lifting the eyes has biblical precedent: "When Solomon had finished praying all this prayer and supplication to Yahweh, he arose from before Yahweh's altar, from kneeling on his knees with his hands spread out toward heaven" (1 Kings 8:54). Posture is not performance—it is agreement between body and spirit.

A pastor I listened to on social media encouraged people to kneel with hands raised in prayer for a week. I followed the advice for about three weeks. Eventually, I thought, "Okay, that was probably enough." But then, that Sunday, the pastor at my own church made a casual remark during service: "Remember to lift your hands when you pray." That was no coincidence. That was a synchronicity—God's way of gently nudging me to keep going.

Before the Holy Spirit began teaching me, I used pre-written prayers, rosaries, and formal language. But now, prayer has become a living conversation. I usually begin with the Lord's Prayer—it's the foundation, the anchor that centers me in His presence. From there, I move into gratitude. I thank Him for the day's events, for the people in my life, for the fact that He even has a purpose for me.

Gratitude is one of the most powerful ways to align with the Holy Spirit. It's how I shift my frequency and create space for God to move through me. Gratitude opens the door for peace and positivity to manifest—not as empty optimism, but as a deep spiritual posture.

After gratitude, I move into intercession. I pray for others, asking the Lord to show me what they need. Sometimes I speak Scripture over them, applying His Word directly to their lives. Other times, I go into spiritual warfare—rebuking demons, breaking strongholds, calling out the spirits that try to bind people: pride, anger, jealousy, grief, trauma. I pray against anything that would try to keep them from walking in freedom. I name it and break it in Jesus' name. This is something I didn't fully understand until the Holy Spirit taught me: it matters that we pray in Jesus's name.

The Authority of Jesus' Name

This isn't a religious tagline we tack onto a prayer. It's a declaration of authority. Yeshua is the Hebrew form of Jesus (from *Yehoshua*), meaning "Yahweh saves." Even His name declares His mission: "You shall call his name Jesus, for it is he who will save his people from their sins" (Matthew 1:21). To pray "in Jesus' name" is to stand in His finished work and to align our requests with His heart, His will, and His mission.

Jesus said, "Whatever you will ask in my name, that will I do, that the Father may be glorified in the Son. If you will ask anything in my name, I will do it" (John 14:13-14). Again, "Whatever you may ask of the Father in my name, he will give it to you" (John 16:23). This is not a formula or incantation;

it is covenant access. We come to the throne not in our own righteousness but through the blood of the Lamb, sealed with the Holy Spirit (Ephesians 1:13).

This is why the name of Jesus carries power in Scripture: "Lord, even the demons are subject to us in your name!" (Luke 10:17); "In the name of Jesus Christ of Nazareth, get up and walk!" (Acts 3:6). God has "highly exalted him, and gave to him the name which is above every name, that at the name of Jesus every knee should bow" (Philippians 2:9-10). The authority of the name flows from being in Him, not merely speaking syllables (see the warning in Acts 19:13-16).

So when I pray for protection, I don't just ask for safety—I declare it in Yeshua's name. When I resist the enemy, I don't do it in my strength—I do it in Jesus' name (James 4:7). He is the One who overcame; He is the reason we have authority at all. This shift turned my prayers from wishful thinking into spiritual action. I stopped wondering if God heard me and began knowing that He does—not because I am perfect or say the right words, but because I come in the name of His Son, and the Father always honors the Son.

Sacrifice as Surrender to God

After that, I offer up sacrifices. Not in the Old Testament sense of burning offerings on an altar, but as a priest of the new covenant—laying down my fears, my doubts, my frustrations. I offer God the parts of me that still feel too heavy to carry. I surrender them at His feet. That's a key part of obedience: not just asking God to fix things, but handing them over. Saying, "This is too big for me. Take it, please."

Surrender isn't about weakness. It's about letting go of our illusion of control. It's choosing to step out into the unknown, trusting that what God has prepared is greater than anything we're leaving behind. Surrender is the door to the journey.

But what happens when we refuse the call?

We see it in Jonah. God asked him to go to Nineveh, but Jonah ran the other way. He boarded a ship, trying to escape the voice of God. But his refusal didn't lead to safety—it led to a storm. He was thrown overboard, swallowed by a great fish, and only after being brought to the brink did he finally surrender. It was in the belly of the whale—his wilderness—that Jonah cried out to God.

Many of us go through this. We sense God calling us to grow, to change, to step into purpose, but fear grips us. Fear of failure. Fear of what people will say. Fear of losing what's familiar. And so we run—into relationships, jobs, addictions, distractions. But just like Jonah, we eventually find ourselves swallowed by something too big to escape. It's there, in that confined place, where we come face to face with God—and with ourselves.

In the hero's journey, refusing the call doesn't cancel the journey. It delays it. Eventually, the path finds us again.

Surrender is the turning point. It's when we stop resisting and start trusting. It's when we say, "Yes, Lord, even if I'm scared. Even if I don't know how this ends. I choose You."

Saying yes to God doesn't just mean going on a new journey—it also means letting go of the old one: the ways we used to think, the habits that no longer serve us, the false identities we clung to. This is where surrender begins to deepen into sacrifice.

Transformation Through Letting Go

Letting go of control is the first step, but transformation often requires placing something meaningful on the altar. Something we didn't want to give up. Something we thought we needed to survive. Saying yes to God is not always about going somewhere—it's about becoming someone. The version of you that can carry Kingdom abundance doesn't come without cost. We must be refined. And sometimes that refining feels like fire.

Paul wrote, "Therefore I urge you, brothers, by the mercies of God, to present your bodies a living sacrifice, holy, acceptable to God, which is your spiritual service" (Romans 12:1). That's not about pain—it's about alignment. It's about laying down what weighs us down so we can rise in freedom.

When I finally understood this, I realized sacrifice was never about loss. It was about trust. It was about agreeing to let the Holy Spirit lead, even when I didn't understand what was happening in the moment. Even if it looked messy. Even if it meant losing control.

That's how transformation happens. Not in the moments where we feel holy and composed, but in the moments where everything feels undone and we still say yes. And after that yes—after the ego dies, after the fear fades, after the tantrum passes—we discover that God was never asking to take from us. He was asking to give us more of Himself.

So I ask Him to reshape my desires. I pray, "Help me to choose what You choose, desire what You desire, and align my will with Your will." Because that's where real transformation happens—not just when we obey, but when our hearts begin to align with His.

Praying for Protection and Guidance

Lastly, I pray for protection. I don't say that lightly. Having been diagnosed with PTSD, I have faced real darkness. I have stared straight into the eyes of evil, and I never want to go back there again. I know what it feels like when the enemy is too close. So I ask the Lord to surround me, cover me, protect me—body, mind, and spirit. I plead the blood of Jesus over my life—not as superstition, but as a shield. Because I know what I'm up against. And I know that only God can keep me safe.

One of those moments came on a simple dog walk. I walk my two large dogs every day, always holding their leashes in my left hand so I can quickly steer them with my right if needed. One day, as we crossed the street toward the park near my home, I felt something—almost like someone was holding my right hand.

At first, I brushed it off. But then I thought, "Okay... I guess we're holding hands." So I shifted my hand into the position as if I were holding someone else's. It felt a little silly, but I wanted to honor the moment—even if quietly. As we walked into the park, out of nowhere, two large German Shepherds appeared. No leashes. No owners in sight.

I had my nine-year-old girl with me on a scooter. My dogs are not especially friendly with other dogs, and now these two shepherds were heading straight for us. My heart dropped.

I told my girl to scoot away and positioned myself near a large tree, so nothing could sneak up from behind. The strange dogs approached—curious, intense. My dogs bristled. It was seconds away from becoming something dangerous. And then, a man I'd never seen before ran up, yelling, and chased the dogs away. They disappeared across the street and into the neighborhood.

In the quiet that followed, I looked up. I thought back to that strange feeling of a hand I'd felt in mine, and I knew. I told God right then, "We are holding hands from now on." That evening, a song came on the radio about holding hands. Of course it did.

Worship as Warfare

Worship isn't mood music for church; it's kingdom warfare. In Scripture, praise is a weapon the Holy Spirit uses to enthrone God's presence, displace darkness, and realign us to heaven's rule. "But you are holy, you who inhabit the praises of Israel" (Psalm 22:3). When God is enthroned in our praise, lesser thrones are toppled.

The significance of worship in spiritual contexts
- **It demonstrates the concept of divine authority.**
  In some traditions, praise is viewed as inviting the

presence and influence of a higher power (referencing Psalm 22:3).
- **It addresses negative influences.** Certain beliefs hold that acts of praise can help counteract opposition or negativity (see Psalm 8:2).
- **It encourages shifts in mindset.** Worship may be associated with letting go of fear, resentment, and excessive self-reliance, and focusing on constructive principles (based on 2 Corinthians 10:4–5).
- **It involves both submission and resistance.** Within certain frameworks, submitting to a higher authority is considered a step toward overcoming challenges (referencing James 4:7).
- **It reflects on themes of victory and testimony.** Some perspectives highlight the importance of narrative and reflection in expressing spiritual triumph (see Revelation 12:11).

Bible snapshots of worship as a weapon:
- Jehoshaphat's singers led the army, and their praise caused God to defeat their enemies (2 Chronicles 20:21–22).
- Jericho's walls fell after obedient marching and a unified shout (Joshua 6:1–20).
- Paul and Silas sang at midnight; God opened prison doors and broke chains (Acts 16:25–26).
- David's harp playing relieved Saul's torment (1 Samuel 16:23).

Kingdom worship changes atmospheres. We sing, play, and declare in Jesus' name, because His is the name above every name (Philippians 2:9-10). Our songs are not incantations; they are covenant allegiance and obedience offered through the blood of the Lamb (John 14:13-14; John 16:23).

What worship does in us (and around us)
- **Shifts desires and emotions:** Praise redirects our focus from fear or cravings to God's sufficiency (Matthew 4:4).
- **Brings joy:** Thanksgiving replaces heaviness with praise (Isaiah 61:3).
- **Breaks chains:** Worship can loosen unseen bonds, even under pressure (Acts 16:25-26).
- **Sharpens discernment:** Focusing on holiness helps us recognize what's false (1 John 4:1).

How to Practice Warfare Worship (Simple Liturgy)
- Give thanks out loud for specific mercies (Psalm 100:4).
- Proclaim Jesus' Lordship and your trust (Philippians 2:9-11).
- Sing Scripture—select a psalm or chorus (Colossians 3:16).
- Testify about what Jesus has done for you (Revelation 12:11).
- Renounce fear and declare God's promises (James 4:7; 2 Corinthians 1:20).

- Pause, listen, and follow one direction from the Holy Spirit (John 14:26; Romans 8:14).

When opposition rises:
- Stay humble and keep praising; don't let worry replace worship.
- Ask a few others to pray with you for greater spiritual authority (Matthew 18:19-20).
- Combine praise with fasting to break unhelpful patterns (Isaiah 58:6).

When Obedience Feels Impossible

Confession: I love, love, love rock 'n' roll: Hard Rock, Alternative, Classic Rock—the works. It helped me survive some hard seasons. So this was not one of those easy obedience moments. The first night I tried to switch, I queued up some Christian rock...and then threw a temper tantrum all night. I did not ask for Christian pop or Christian country. I wanted rock. I wanted my rock.

Still, I endured. I was determined to find something I could handle and I kept the playlist on. Later that night an ad on that new playlist popped up with the message, "God thanks you for listening to His music." I burst out laughing with the Lord, because He and I both knew how hard that was for me—and how dramatic my tantrum had been.

How can you not fall in love with Him when He encourages and supports you like that?

Obedience didn't start with a feeling; it started with a yes. And God met me there with kindness. "For it is God who works in you both to will and to work, for his good pleasure" (Philippians 2:13).

Even in music, obedience is relationship. Sometimes the Holy Spirit asks us to change what we sing so He can change what we believe. The new soundtrack didn't erase my love for rock—but over time I found more songs that have since grown on me. And the lyrics I sing started writing truth into my heart, and worship became warfare that actually worked.

Worship as Warfare: Why Your Soundtrack Matters

What we sing is never neutral. Lyrics become agreements; melodies become memory hooks that train the heart. Scripture says, "Death and life are in the power of the tongue" (Proverbs 18:21), "give no place to the devil" (Ephesians 4:27), and "Keep your heart with all diligence, for out of it is the wellspring of life" (Proverbs 4:23). In Bible language, your mouth and your meditations are gates (Psalm 19:14). Worship is warfare because it enthrones God's rule in those gates (Psalm 22:3).

How lyrics become footholds (the agreement pathway)

- **Exposure → Meditation.** What we loop in our ears we begin to ponder (Psalm 1:2).
- **Meditation → Confession.** We start repeating the phrases; "out of the abundance of the heart, his mouth speaks" (Luke 6:45).
- **Confession → Agreement.** Repeated words function like micro-vows; they can legitimize envy,

lust, revenge, despair, or self-exaltation (James 3:5–6).
- **Agreement → Atmosphere.** Agreements invite either the Holy Spirit's fruit (Galatians 5:22–23) or a "spirit of heaviness"—dense emotions and negative self-talk (Isaiah 61:3).

Three tests for any song
- **Word test (Philippians 4:8):** Is it true, honorable, pure, lovely?
- **Fruit test (James 2:17 / Galatians 5:22–23):** Does it stir faith, love, self-control—or fuel fleshly appetites?
- **Authority test (John 14:13–14):** Can I sing/say this in Jesus' name with a clean conscience?

Not every secular song is sinful; not every "Christian" lyric is wise. Test the spirits (1 John 4:1).

Practicing worship-warfare with your music
- **Curate your soundscape.** Build playlists of psalms, hymns, Christ-exalting songs for morning, work, and night. Lower the ambient noise that stokes fear, lust, rage, or self-pity (Psalm 101:3).
- **Sing Scripture.** Put short verses to melody (e.g., Psalm 23; Psalm 27:1; Romans 8:1). Melody helps truth stick.
- **Renounce & replace (out loud).** "In Jesus' name I renounce the lie that I am abandoned." "I agree with

Your Word: 'He will never leave me nor forsake me' (Hebrews 13:5)."
- **Use worship as a shield.** When heaviness hits, lift a "midnight song" like Paul and Silas (Acts 16:25–26). Praise precedes the breakthrough.
- **Guard your confessions.** Avoid "singing your sins" as identity (Ephesians 4:29). Confess sin to God (1 John 1:9), but don't glorify it in melody.
- **Linking back to obedience and manifesting with the Holy Spirit**
- **Obedience:** Choosing what you sing is a daily *yes* to God's wisdom (John 10:27). Kneeling, raising hands, declaring in Jesus' name—these are obedient postures, not theatrics.
- **Authority:** We pray and sing **in Jesus' name**, approaching the Father through the Son (John 16:23). Authority flows from covenant, not from catchy words.
- **Manifestation (Kingdom style):** What you agree with becomes visible. As you enthrone Jesus with your words and songs, the Spirit forms His fruit, frees captives, and aligns circumstances with the Father's will (John 15:7–8; 2 Corinthians 10:5). We're not "attracting" outcomes by vibration; we're cooperating with the Holy Spirit until heaven's will takes shape on earth.

A 7-day "playlist audit" (quick plan)
- **Day 1:** List your top 20 songs. Mark themes (hope/despair, purity/lust, humility/pride).
- **Day 2:** Cut 25% that fail the Word/Fruit/Authority tests.
- **Day 3:** Add 5 Scripture songs; sing one morning and night.
- **Day 4:** Replace passive listening with 10 minutes of sung prayer.
- **Day 5:** Renounce one recurring lie; write a Scripture chorus that answers it.
- **Day 6:** Invite a friend to agree and worship with you (Matthew 18:19–20).
- **Day 7:** Journal the change in atmosphere, thoughts, and choices (Romans 12:2).

Bottom line: Your mouth is a source of power; your playlist is a liturgy. Close the gate of your mind to lies; open it to truth. Worship as warfare—in Jesus' name—shifts agreements, breaks footholds, and makes room for the Holy Spirit to manifest the Father's will in your life.

How This Relates to Manifesting with the Holy Spirit

Manifesting with the Holy Spirit isn't forcing reality with technique; it's the Father's will becoming visible in our lives through union with Jesus, alignment with His Word, and obedient steps empowered by the Holy Spirit. "If you remain in me, and my words remain in you, ask whatever you desire, and it will be done for you" (John 15:7).

Kingdom Flow: Steps of Obedience
- **Ask in Jesus' name:** Present requests according to Jesus' authority and purpose, not personal impulse.
- **Align with Scripture:** Let God's Word shape faith and replace false beliefs.
- **Worship as warfare:** Praise establishes God's presence and resists the enemy.
- **Follow Holy Spirit nudges:** Take action—repent, forgive, or create—as evidence of faith.
- **Persevere through hardship:** Continue trusting and obeying during challenging times for spiritual growth.
- **Bear lasting fruit:** True results are seen in freedom, healing, provision, reconciliation, and holy character that honor God.

Jesus' name, worship, and obedience enable manifestation
- **Legal standing:** Approaching the Father in Jesus' name relies on his completed work (John 16:23).
- **Atmospheric rule:** Worship invites God's authority into our minds and lives (Psalm 22:3; Acts 16:25-26).
- **Lived alignment:** Obedience aligns us with the Spirit, rejecting evil and making room for God's will (Romans 8:14; Matthew 6:10).

One sentence: Manifesting with the Holy Spirit is obedient agreement—asking in Jesus' name, enthroning Jesus through worship, and taking Spirit-led steps until the Father's will becomes visible in real life.

Obedience as Relationship, Not Rule

Obedience isn't about rules. It's about relationship. It's about learning to recognize the signs, to respond to the nudges, to take God's hand even when we're scared. He doesn't command obedience for His sake—but for ours. So He can guide us, protect us, grow us, and yes—walk with us through the unknown.

Sometimes obedience is learning to pray differently. Other times, it's being asked to kneel when no one else around you is kneeling. Or to raise your hands when you don't feel like it. It's spiritual training. Coachability. It's learning how to move in rhythm with the Holy Spirit.

Obedience doesn't mean perfection. It means willingness. Willing to listen. Willing to try. Willing to have conversations with the Holy Spirit. Willing to hold His hand when you don't know what's coming next.

Jesus said, "My sheep hear my voice, and I know them, and they follow me" (John 10:27). Obedience helps you learn that voice. Not just in moments of crisis—but in every ordinary step, even on a quiet walk to the park.

And this is where relationship deepens: when obedience moves from rare moments of surrender into a daily rhythm of seeking God's face. We open His Word to hear Him. We pray not just when we are desperate, but because we long for His presence. We cultivate quiet moments with Him like we would with a trusted friend. In this way, obedience becomes the pathway to intimacy, and intimacy fuels obedience.

To walk with God is to seek Him every day—in Scripture, in prayer, and in relationship—until obedience is no longer a burden, but a joy.

Chapter Nine

Repentance is Raw

Repentance isn't pretty. It isn't inspirational. It's the moment you stop protecting your image and say what's true. If I'm going to stand in front of anyone and show them how to do it, I have to be honest about what it costs. No one likes repentance. No one likes admitting they were wrong. And when you finally say, "I was wrong," the world will often weaponize that one confession and try to make it your whole identity—"See? You're always wrong."

That's how it felt when my daughter died. It became proof, to them and to me, that I'd been wrong all along. It was as if every choice I'd made up to that point collapsed in one day. It sounded like all the old voices were right—the ones that said a single mom doesn't get to have a life, that I should've stayed in my lane, that trying to outthink the system would only end badly. I could hear the chorus: *We told you so.* Repentance, for me, started there—not with a tidy lesson, but with the weight of that accusation sitting in my chest while I said out loud what I didn't want to say: I don't have this figured out. I am not the hero of this story. I need mercy.

This is the ground floor. No gloss. No bright side. Just the truth, and a heart willing to be broken before God, because "a broken and contrite heart, O God, you will not despise" (Psalm 51:17).

Learning the Game

I graduated into the wreckage. The 2008 recession slammed Colorado in 2010, and that's where I learned what "survival of the fittest" actually means. I was competing with professionals for unpaid internships that went nowhere. To prove I wasn't idle, I paid for daycare so I could work for free. Net negative.

Employers got creative: the group interview. Fifty of us in a room, taking turns at a microphone to explain why we deserved the job more than everyone else—knowing they had two more rooms just like ours waiting after we finished. I couldn't win in that arena. So I did the only thing I knew: I went back to school to keep the aid and the loans coming, just to stay afloat.

Meanwhile, the world kept telling me I wasn't good enough—because I was a single mom on welfare. The names stuck: trash, burden, ride-me-hard-and-put-me-away-wet. Two years passed before I landed a full-time job, at the most volatile place I've ever worked: a bank. Hidden agendas. Jealousy. Politicking. Backstabbing. Gossip. Smiles like masks. Whatever you did, it wasn't enough.

I still moved from teller to supervisor in about eighteen months. My method was simple: fists clenched in an empty break room, breathe, walk back out, survive the day. And you never tell the next employer the truth about the last place.

You smile through your teeth and give a clean reason you're "seeking new opportunities."

In a world of shifting appearances, you don't make it by telling the truth.

Dating, Reduced to Math

They say don't hate the player, hate the game. I didn't hate either. I learned the rules and tried to play them better than everyone else.

With daycare due, bills stacked, income unstable, support thin, and loans coming due, you don't date for love. If you do, men scatter like you're contagious. You look for an exchange: he needs something you can give; he can provide something you need. He has two kids who need a mom; I have a kid who needs to be picked up after school so I can work full-time. I have an apartment; he has disability. He can't work; I have to work. It isn't romance; it's a transaction. It's survival in a concrete world.

That's where the fights outside the home start. Friends still think you should wait for the one you're "in love with," as if that kind of safety is waiting at the end of a bar tab. They're not paying for childcare. They want you out to dance, to be their entertainment, to prove you're "fun." Family wants the old version of you—the one who bent over backward to meet their needs—no matter what it costs you now.

So you bargain. You budget your heart. You measure affection in rent money and rides and who's home by six. You learn to keep your face straight when the math doesn't add up. And you tell yourself this is how it has always been, why history is full of arranged marriages. This is what my ancestors did, this is what I do.

Winning at What Cost?

Four years after my first degree, after the recession hangover and all the hustling, loss hit close. My stepfather fell from a 14er and died on impact. We identified his body with his head covered because animals had gotten there before search and rescue could bring him down. Two of my six siblings were in active addiction. There's no manual for that—only family fights, lies, finger-pointing, enabling, kids in the middle. Surviving it once didn't make the second round easier.

Then a door finally opened: a property claims adjuster job. Three months of paid training and licensing. A real starting salary. I told myself I wouldn't be "scum" anymore. I had played the game and won.

On paper, yes. At night, I stood under the shower and cried to rinse off the day. The win had a price: years of grinding and strategizing, smiling through lies, clenching my fists in break rooms, outlasting gossip and doubt. I kept telling myself I'd made it.

I had—if that's what winning is.

Human beings are resilient. Made in God's image, we can carry more than seems possible. I did. But there's a cost to white-knuckling your way through life.

I thought I had the world figured out—until, six months after that "win," the rug yanked out from under me and suddenly the world didn't make sense. Pink didn't mean pink; it meant fork. Fork didn't mean fork; it meant turn left.

People get uncomfortable with anger. I didn't. Anger was the fuel that kept me moving for years. I said it often: depression and fear don't make a woman leave an abusive relationship—anger does. Low self-esteem doesn't make a broke student grind—anger does. Societies don't change until they're angry. For me, anger wasn't the problem; it was the engine. Then I learned there's one thing that makes people more uncomfortable than anger: the death of a child.

Days after her passing, the rumors started—whispers that my fiancé or my stepson must have killed her, as if I'd invited a murderer into my home. Life—and everyone in it—became a *Criminal Minds* episode. Worse, I couldn't find gravity: I didn't know up from down or fact from fiction.

People opted not to talk directly to me because they "didn't want to remind" me. I would walk into the grocery store: my daughter died. Pull out a cart: my daughter died. First aisle: my daughter died. Dairy section: my daughter died. Pick up a package of cheese: my daughter died. as if I could ever forget for one moment.

The women I'd called second mothers went silent. I was furious when my canceled wedding day turned into a baby shower on social media for someone else—posted by people I'd invited to my ceremony. Babies were arriving everywhere when mine was gone.

At work, I had only been there six months. Do you know what it feels like to watch twelve people from your training class get promoted because their children are still alive and they don't breakdown in grief attacks throughout the day? I do.

Do you know what it feels like to pack up your house five months after you bury your only child due to the landlord wanting to sell "because a child died there"? I do.

Do you know what it's like when new people ask if you have kids and every time you have to choose between lying or making them uncomfortable with the truth? I do.

Do you know what it's like to stand in a baby shower and keep quiet because nobody wants to hear labor stories from a mother whose child is dead? I do.

Underneath the fury was a heavier thing: the sense that God was punishing me—maybe for how I handled my family members' addictions, because I drew lines and refused to enable. Guilt pressed like a weight on my chest. Shame rewrote my name. It felt like the whole world had watched God make an example out of me. Yeah, been there, done that.

A Call for Repentance

Repentance is another one of those scary words—especially when we hear it through the filter of religion, shame, or fear. For many of us, it's wrapped in images of punishment or penance, as if we have to crawl our way back to God's favor. But repentance isn't groveling. It's healing. It's clearing blockages in the soul so communion with God can be restored.

In the Catholic faith, we have contrition and confession. For most of my life, that was how I understood repentance: feel bad, confess to a priest, receive penance. After my daughter died, I didn't go to confession for almost nine years. When God called me to repent in November 2024, my mind went straight back to the rulebook: schedule a time with a priest, do it the right way.

So I reached out—voicemail, email, followed the website instructions. Nothing. No reply. No follow-up.

At first, I felt abandoned. Then the Holy Spirit showed me something else: I didn't need a human intercessor to pour out my heart to God. Jesus had made the way. I could repent directly to the Father. I brought Him my grief, my anger, my confusion. I asked my questions. I shed my tears. And I named the thing He put His finger on: it wasn't wrong to feel angry; it was wrong that I let anger choose silence.

The very women I once called second mothers later buried their adult children because of alcoholism. When they did, I didn't extend an olive branch. I let them feel the weight they'd left me to carry.

One of those mothers eventually drank herself into a nursing home. Near the end she grew delirious, convinced the nurses meant her harm. A few months after I repented, God handed me a chance to do the thing I hadn't done before: show mercy. I sat on the phone and soothed her until her son could reach the facility and sort it out.

Forgiveness: Handing Back the Gavel

Forgiveness isn't sentimental. It's surgical. It's the decision to stop trying cases in your head at 2 a.m. and hand the gavel back to God. Scripture is blunt: "Vengeance belongs to me; I will repay, says the Lord" (Romans 12:19). If vengeance is His, it can't be mine—not even in the courtroom of my thoughts.

Unforgiveness is heavy. It's dense. It drags the soul into a low frequency where bitterness breeds (Hebrews 12:15), where anger goes from momentary to malignant and gives the enemy a foothold (Ephesians 4:26-27). In that density, prayer feels jammed and worship feels thin. Jesus ties unclogged prayer directly to forgiveness: before you ask, forgive (Mark 11:25). This isn't God being harsh; it's God protecting your signal. Forgiveness lifts you back into alignment with the Holy Spirit's movement—what I call heaven's frequency.

King David didn't bottle it up or pretty it up. He said it to God. He filed his case upward so vengeance could stay where it belongs.

- "Pour out your heart before him. God is a refuge for us." (Psalm 62:8)
- "I pour out my complaint before him. I tell him my troubles." (Psalm 142:2)
- "How long, Yahweh? Will you forget me forever?" (Psalm 13:1)
- "In return for my love, they are my adversaries; but I am in prayer." (Psalm 109:4)
- "Cast your burden on Yahweh, and he will sustain you." (Psalm 55:22)

David brought the whole thing—rage, fear, accusations, names, details—and he brought it **to** God. That's not venting; that's worshipful honesty. It keeps me from triangulating people into my pain or recruiting allies for revenge. When I talk it out with God, I'm handing the gavel back: "Vengeance belongs to me; I will repay, says the Lord" (Romans 12:19).

This is how I practice it now: I say exactly what happened and exactly how it feels, the way David did. I ask for justice, protection, and clean hands. I end where David usually ends—trust. Not because the feeling is resolved, but because the matter is in the right court. And that shift matters. Unforgiveness drags me into a dense place where bitterness breeds; voicing the grievance to God clears the air, keeps my heart soft, and helps me stay in the Holy Spirit's flow—what I call heaven's frequency—so my prayers aren't jammed and my worship isn't thin (Mark 11:25).

David teaches me that forgiveness doesn't start with pretending I'm fine. It starts with telling God the truth, then letting Him carry what I can't.

Secondly, when I say, "I hereby release the debt owed," I'm not pretending the loss was small. I'm acting under the authority of a King who cancels accounts. Jesus told of a ruler who forgave a servant an impossible sum—ten thousand talents—simply because the man pleaded for mercy (Matthew 18:23-27). The point wasn't the servant's worthiness; it was the king's authority to wipe the ledger clean.

In the same way, when I release someone from **my** claim, I'm exercising delegated authority as a subject of that King. I cancel what I am owed at the personal level and hand ultimate justice to God. Jesus said, "Whatever you bind on earth will have been bound in heaven, and whatever you release on earth will have been released in heaven"

(Matthew 18:18). So forgiveness is not vague positivity; it's a real act of release that aligns earth with heaven's court.

Here's how to practice forgiveness in real life—no glow, just grit:
- **Name it plainly.** Say what happened and what it cost. No minimizing. No spin (Psalm 51:6).
- **Return the gavel.** Out loud: "Father, vengeance is Yours, not mine (Romans 12:19). I release judgment to You."
- **Forgive as an act, not a feeling.** "I forgive __ for __. This is the debt they owe me: __. I hereby release the debt owed." Feelings may lag; the decision stands (Matthew 6:12, 14–15).
- **Ask for cleansing and re-alignment.** "Search me... and lead me in the everlasting way" (Psalm 139:23-24).
- **Hold your boundaries.** As far as it depends on you, live at peace (Romans 12:18) without re-entering harm.

When I do this, I'm not "being positive." I'm choosing not to carry a weight God has claimed as His. Forgiveness is how I keep my heart from hardening and my signal from clogging. It's how I stay in the atmosphere where grace actually moves—where prayer in Yeshua's name is more than words, and worship becomes warfare that doesn't boomerang back on me.

Bottom line: Forgiveness is not letting anyone off the hook. It's taking yourself off the hook of vengeance so your soul can rise to the frequency of heaven, where the Holy Spirit leads, heals, and speaks.

The Lazarus Question

One day I watched a sermon about Lazarus from Elevation Church. The pastor read Martha's words to Jesus: "Therefore Martha said to Jesus, 'Lord, if you would have been here, my brother wouldn't have died'" (John 11:21). He asked us to name our own "if You had been here" moment.

I knew mine. When my daughter died, I canceled my wedding to pay for her funeral. I carried that resentment quietly for years, never daring to say it out loud: *God, why would You rather have a funeral than a wedding?*

As Pastor Furtick continued, tears poured. In my mind's eye, I saw a warm orange light enter my chest like a weld closing a fracture. The Holy Spirit was healing something I couldn't reach on my own.

Repentance, Washing, and the War in the Mind

Repentance isn't just saying "sorry." It's a washing—a real cleanse that happens as the Holy Spirit runs the Word through our thoughts until they're clean again. Scripture calls it "the washing of water with the word" (Ephesians 5:26) and commands us to be "transformed by the renewing of your mind" (Romans 12:2). That's the battleground: the mind.

Sin doesn't start with the act; it starts as a thought that we either reject or enter into agreement with. James says desire "conceives" and then "gives birth to sin" (James 1:14–

15). So the enemy works upstream—at conception—through lies and accusations. After the Cross, Jesus "stripped the principalities and the powers" and triumphed over them (Colossians 2:15). What remains as the enemy's primary weapons are deception and accusation—he is "a liar and the father of it" (John 8:44) and "the accuser of our brothers" (Revelation 12:10).

Repentance answers both. When a lie slips in and we start agreeing with it, repentance breaks that agreement and replaces it with truth. When accusation hammers us, repentance brings us back under what Jesus has already done—cleansed, covered, and re-aligned (1 John 1:9).

Here's how I practice it in real life without theatrics: I name the agreement—out loud. I renounce it. Then I replace it with the Word. For example: "I renounce the lie that I'm condemned; in Jesus, there is now no condemnation" (Romans 8:1). That's not positive thinking; that's wielding "the sword of the Spirit, which is the word of God" (Ephesians 6:17) while taking thoughts captive to obey Christ (2 Corinthians 10:5). It's a rinse-and-repeat rhythm: repent, renounce, replace, renew—as many times as it takes until the loop breaks and peace returns.

About the critique I've heard—"Catholics think they can sin, ask forgiveness, then go do it again." No. God is not fooled. "Yahweh looks at the heart" (1 Samuel 16:7). He receives a "broken and contrite heart" (Psalm 51:17), and it's His kindness that leads to repentance, not a license to keep sinning (Romans 2:4). Grace doesn't make sin safer; grace trains us: "the grace of God... instructs us to deny ungodliness" (Titus 2:11–12). Is anyone practicing perfectly?

No. That's why grace exists—to pardon and empower. But treating grace like permission is self-deception; treating grace like power is transformation.

So when intrusive thoughts hit, when old agreements try to reattach, when shame replays the past: I wash again. I let the Word run over the wound. I admit where I entertained the lie. I turn—back into truth, back into Jesus. Repentance isn't groveling; it's maintenance. It keeps the channel clear so the Holy Spirit can renew what the lie tried to rewrite.

Armor & Anthems: Breaking the Thought Loop with Worship

Intrusive, perseverating thoughts can feel like torture—PTSD turns a passing phrase into a stuck record. I've had a throwaway jab ("who do you think you are, Oreo Big Stuff?") loop in my head for hours. After the 2016 Colorado hailstorm shredded my house, I uploaded a photo to Sherwin-Williams and "painted" it every color for nearly two months—every break, every lunch, late nights—circling the drain because I couldn't decide. My ex-fiancé finally chose for me. I wish I'd known then what I know now: after repentance, when the slate is clean and the enemy tries to pull you back down with mental loops, apply the lessons from Chapters three and seven: put on your armor—and turn up the worship. Why this works (biblically):

- We're not wrestling people; this is spiritual (Ephesians 6:12).

- Armor guards your mind and heart: the helmet of salvation, shield of faith, breastplate of righteousness (Ephesians 6:13–17).
- God is *enthroned on the praises of Israel*—praise shifts the atmosphere (Psalm 22:3).
- Praise is warfare: singers went before the army and God scattered the enemy (2 Chronicles 20:21–22); Paul and Silas sang, and prison doors opened (Acts 16:25–26).
- We take thoughts captive and make them obey Christ (2 Corinthians 10:5), and we **set** our minds on what is true (Philippians 4:8).

The 5-Minute "Armor & Anthems" drill

1. **Name the loop.** Out loud and plain: "This thought is a lie/accusation/fear." (Psalm 51:6)
2. **Armor up.**
   - *Helmet of salvation:* "Jesus, save my mind; I belong to You."
   - *Breastplate of righteousness:* "I am covered in Your righteousness, not my performance."
   - *Shield of faith:* "I quench every flaming arrow of accusation." (Ephesians 6:16)
   - *Belt of truth / shoes of peace:* "Secure me in Your Word; steady me in Your peace."
   - *Sword of the Spirit:* speak a verse that counters the loop (e.g., Philippians 4:6–8; Romans 8:1).
3. **Hit play.** Put on worship that declares Scripture (identity in Christ, the blood of Jesus, God's

faithfulness). Keep it Christ-centered, not just "uplifting." (Psalm 22:3)
4. **Sing/declare with your body.** Stand up. Open your hands. If you can, dance—even small steps. Movement helps interrupt the loop. *"To appoint... the garment of praise for the spirit of heaviness."* (Isaiah 61:3)
5. **Swap the script.** "In Yeshua's name, I reject __; I receive Your truth: __." (John 14:13–14; 2 Corinthians 10:5)
6. **Breathe a short prayer.** Inhale: "Jesus, have mercy." Exhale: "Rule in my mind." Repeat for one song.
7. **If the loop returns, repeat.** You're training reflexes, not chasing a feeling (Ephesians 6:13).

After repentance, it's normal for old grooves to try to re-etch themselves. Worship is not denial; it's defiance—placing God on the throne of your thought-life when accusation demands the seat. If you're dealing with PTSD, keep using wise supports (therapy, grounding tools, care team) *alongside* worship. The Holy Spirit uses means.

I'd catch the obsession early and run the drill. I'd put on a Christ-centered playlist, stand up, and sing until my breathing matched the truth again. I'd ask, "Holy Spirit, is there a simple next step?" Then I'd make one small decision and log off. No more two-month spiral. Armor on. Music up. Eyes on Jesus.

Because when the tempting thoughts come—especially right after a clean slate—the response is not to white-knuckle the mind. It's to worship as warfare, let the Word fight for you, and keep your soul in the Holy Spirit's steady rhythm until the loop breaks.

What Manifesting with the Holy Spirit Means

This is one of the most amazing results of manifesting with the Holy Spirit. Not wealth. Not power. Not prestige. Healing. A renewed mind. A soul that has gone to war with the lies it learned from a dishonest world.

It looks like keeping your eyes on Jesus when the waves say you're going under. It looks like repentance and forgiveness clearing the channel so grace can move.

Do you always feel it? No. I quit my most recent job to follow Jesus, and today all the bills came due. I don't know how I'm going to pay them. The positive-affirmation videos on social media tell me to stay upbeat, retrain my subconscious, and break agreements with the enemy. Some of that helps. It only goes so far.

So here I am, writing this after walking my dogs with tears streaming down my face, thinking: here we go again. The temptation is to start hustling and grinding to make rent in two weeks. Everyone says God will provide if you do His work—that He goes before you and that when you step into the Jordan, the water stops at the exact moment. Then I recognize old negative energy bubbling to the surface, the uncharacteristic emotion. I'm on the precipice of another breakthrough.

I don't have a bow to tie on this. I have repentance. I have a phone call I answered when mercy was required. I have a question I finally asked God out loud. I have a heart that's still breaking and a Savior who still hears. I get up dust myself off and endure because we are not always going to feel like it, sometimes it doesn't even look like it's going to happen and all those negative self-talk thoughts threaten to flood back in. For today, though that's what obedience looks like. That's what love looks like. That's what faith looks like. And when I doubt or fear, that's what repentance is for.

Chapter Ten

Loving God's New Creation

For many years, I didn't have a lot of people pouring kind words or encouragement into me. I fell into the trap of always giving, always showing up, always carrying the load for others—but I didn't really know how to receive. Somewhere along the way, I confused sacrifice with purpose.

I think part of it came from how I was raised. In my family, both my brother and my sister carried the same idea: that we were supposed to model our lives after Jesus. Maybe it was from staring at Him hanging on the cross in church, or maybe it was the rhythm of Lent each year—but we all internalized this image that being like Jesus meant suffering, sacrificing, and fighting the devil ourselves.

It wasn't until we got older—after branching into other denominations through marriage and new churches—that I began to hear something different. Pastors started teaching that the battle with the enemy belongs to God, not us. That we're called to receive from Him. That He saves, He provides, He fights.

At first, I was dumbfounded. If God was supposed to do everything, then what was left for me to do? What was the point of my life? The answer, surprisingly, was plenty. But it wasn't the "plenty" I expected. It wasn't more striving, more giving, more bleeding myself dry. It was about living as a daughter, not a savior. It was about setting boundaries, not burning out. It was about resting, not constantly warring.

Looking back, I realize that I put myself in places I didn't belong because I thought I had to be the one to fix everything. I thought it was my responsibility to save, to fight, to provide, to give, to sacrifice. But all it did was overspend my energy. There were no boundaries. There was no Sabbath rest. There was never any time to breathe, to recover, to let God refill me.

However, choosing Jesus is choosing life—your life. The one He designed. The one He dreamed into existence before you were even born. The one He paid for with His own blood. When you say yes to Him, you're not erasing your identity. You're finally stepping into it.

Since inviting the Holy Spirit into my life, things have become increasingly fantastic. And I don't mean in the superficial sense of sunshine and rainbows. I mean fantastic in the literal sense—like something out of a novel or movie. Every day feels like an adventure, full of meaning, symbols, synchronicities, and sacred nudges. Some days are quiet. Some days are hard. But all of them are woven with purpose.

Liking Yourself ≠ Loving Yourself

I used to think I had this part down. I didn't hate myself. I could list things I liked: my humor on good days, my work ethic on bad ones. So when people kept saying, "You have to love yourself before you can be in a relationship," I rolled my eyes. Cringe. Another clip about "choosing yourself," "pouring into your own cup," "healing through self-love." I'd think, *I like myself just fine—can I just skip to the good part?*

Here's what I didn't see: liking is a feeling; loving is a choice.

Liking comes and goes with mood, performance, numbers on a scale, numbers in a bank account. Loving is a covenantal stance—choosing care, truth, and honor even on the days you don't like what you see. Jesus tied this to how we treat others: "You shall love your neighbor as yourself" (Mark 12:31). That assumes a baseline of healthy self-regard. If I starve the person God entrusted to me—me—what exactly am I giving my neighbor?

The Holy Spirit started pressing on that difference. Loving myself wasn't indulgence; it was stewardship—honoring the temple where God chose to dwell (1 Corinthians 6:19–20), guarding the wellspring so the water doesn't run muddy (Proverbs 4:23). Jesus said it this way: "The good man out of his good treasure brings out good things, and the evil man out of his evil treasure brings out evil things" (Matthew 12:35). If my heart is empty, tired, or fractured, what treasure do I have to bring out? Liking myself did nothing to refill that storehouse. Loving myself—God's way—meant tending it.

Practically, this is what shifted:
- Thoughts. Liking says, *I feel okay today.* Loving says, *Even if I don't, I will speak truth over me because God does* (Psalm 139:14; Romans 8:1).
- Words. Liking compliments myself on good days. Loving refuses casual self-cursing on bad ones and blesses what God blesses (Psalm 103:1–5).

- Boundaries. Liking gives myself treats. Loving sets limits that protect the image of God in me—even if someone is disappointed (Romans 12:18; Matthew 10:14).
- Correction. Liking avoids discomfort. Loving invites, "Search me, God," because identity is anchored in grace, not performance (Psalm 139:23-24; 1 John 1:9).

I didn't have to manufacture warm feelings. I had to agree with God about my worth in Jesus and treat myself accordingly. That shift didn't make me self-centered; it made me usable. When I loved myself as stewardship—rested, told the truth, held boundaries, received correction—the "treasure" in the storehouse actually grew. And from that place, I finally had something real to give away.

Self-Love vs. Pride

Real self-love isn't self-worship; it's consent. It's agreeing with God about who you are in Jesus and then treating yourself accordingly. Scripture gives the shape of that consent: "We are his workmanship, created in Christ Jesus for good works" (Ephesians 2:10). "There is therefore now no condemnation to those who are in Christ Jesus" (Romans 8:1). Holy self-love receives identity as a gift and lives from it. Pride does something else. Sometimes it puffs up—"I am my own source." Sometimes it caves in—"I am trash." Either way, the self stays at the center. Love recenters God. "Love... doesn't brag, is not proud" (1 Corinthians 13:4).

And we are told to "think reasonably" about ourselves, not more highly than we ought (Romans 12:3).

When I practice holy self-love, I'm not inflating my ego; I'm agreeing with what God has already said. If He calls me beloved, I act like someone He loves. That changes my inner talk—no secret self-abuse disguised as honesty—and it changes my choices: rest when He says rest, repent when He puts His finger on something, set boundaries that honor His image in me. "Bless Yahweh, my soul... who crowns you with loving kindness and tender mercies" (Psalm 103:1–4). This is stewardship, not self-sovereignty. My body, time, and gifts are His (1 Corinthians 6:19–20), so I don't lend them to what defaces Him. And because grace is my anchor, correction doesn't destroy me. I can pray, "Search me, God," and repent without self-hatred, trusting His cleansing (Psalm 139:23–24; 1 John 1:9). Love grows fruit; pride curates an image. If what I'm calling "self-love" makes me harsher, stingier, or less truthful, I've drifted from the Spirit's orchard (Galatians 5:22–23).

Pride is crafty enough to dress like care. It whispers, *I owe no one anything, including God; my truth is my law.* Or it says, *My pain permits me to harm others and ignore conviction; I'm the exception.* Sometimes it turns inward and becomes a judge: *If I can't be perfect, I'll punish myself.* These aren't opposite problems; they are the same gravity—me at the center. Holy love breaks that orbit and pulls me into God's. Paradoxically, that's what makes me safer to others. "You shall love your neighbor as yourself" (Mark 12:31) assumes I won't starve the person God has entrusted to my care while trying to feed the world.

I test myself with simple questions, not to condemn but to recalibrate. What is the voice in my head like—accusatory, or shepherding? Jesus says, "My sheep hear my voice" (John 10:27), and His voice doesn't traffic in condemnation (Romans 8:1). Who is at the center of my decisions—my image, or the magnifying of Jesus? "Oh magnify Yahweh with me" (Psalm 34:3). What happens when I am corrected—do I harden, or become teachable, as wisdom invites (Proverbs 9:8–9)? And when I'm done with "self-care," what's left in my wake—more peace, patience, and kindness, or just more defensiveness (Galatians 5:22–23)?

In practice, holy self-love looks like blessing what God blesses. I speak life over my mind and body with Scripture, not because words are magic, but because the Word tells the truth about me when my feelings don't. I keep boundaries that are honest and kind; "as much as it is possible... be at peace with all men" (Romans 12:18) sometimes means shaking the dust off and moving on (Matthew 10:14). I confess quickly and without contempt—repentance as maintenance, not self-loathing (Psalm 51:17). I serve someone quietly where no one sees, because pride starves in hidden faithfulness (Matthew 6:3–4). And when my self-talk starts to spiral, I worship. God is enthroned on praise (Psalm 22:3); pride dims under that light.

This is not cosmetic; it's protective. When I love myself **in Christ**, the enemy's lies have less to stick to. Accusation tells me, *You are your worst moment.* Holy love answers with the Word: "If anyone is in Christ, he is a new creation" (2 Corinthians 5:17). Comparison says, *You're not enough.* Holy love replies, "My grace is sufficient for you; for my power is made perfect in weakness" (2 Corinthians 12:9). That is how self-love becomes armor—keeping me in agreement with God so I don't sign the enemy's contracts, and keeping my heart clear enough to love my neighbor as myself.

Self-Love as Spiritual Protection

I noticed a pattern: the days I refused to value myself the way God does were the days the enemy's lies landed hardest. When I didn't stand in who I was in Christ, accusation had Velcro.

Scripture names a different center of gravity. "We are his workmanship, created in Christ Jesus for good works" (Ephesians 2:10). Identity first, assignment second. That's the air my soul is meant to breathe. And because the heart is the wellspring, it must be guarded: "Keep your heart with all diligence, for out of it is the wellspring of life" (Proverbs 4:23).

Here's how I'm learning to define self-love now: consenting to God's truth about who I am in Jesus, and treating myself accordingly—in my thoughts, in my words, and in my boundaries. I used to think I was choosing Jesus over myself. I thought that when I walked away from old habits, old dreams, or old relationships, I was sacrificing my desires for His. But what I didn't see at first was that choosing Jesus was choosing the "I am" in Him. Not the old me—the one who was afraid of being judged, or who didn't know how to rest in God's timing—but the new me. The one being made new every day by the Holy Spirit. It is not self-worship. It's stewardship of a life the Father loves, redeemed by the Son, and indwelt by the Holy Spirit.

When I don't consent to that truth, I start making quiet agreements with lies. They rarely announce themselves. They slide in as comparisons, as "not enough," as "too much," as the old label I said I'd outgrown. The enemy's tried but true tools after the Cross are deception and accusation; he aims them at the mind and waits for my amen. The Holy Spirit counters with witness and Word, but He doesn't override my will. I still choose whom to agree with.

Words matter. I stopped cursing myself in casual sentences—*I'm so stupid, I always mess this up, of course this would happen to me.* They sound small, but they train the heart to expect condemnation. If Yahweh does not condemn me in Christ, I am not authorized to condemn myself. Agreement begins or ends on my tongue.

And then there are boundaries. Loving myself in Christ means I do not lend the image of God in me to what defaces it. Sometimes the most spiritual sentence I can say is a quiet, "No." Not to punish anyone, but to guard the wellspring so I can say "Yes" where God actually assigned me. If love of neighbor is the command, self-contempt won't get me there. "You shall love your neighbor as yourself" (Mark 12:31) assumes I will not starve the person God has entrusted to my care—me—while trying to feed the world.

Even the data backs this up: compassion toward yourself—God's way—buffers anxiety and keeps shame from hijacking repentance. It's not ego inflation (which research links to fragility); it's the steady, Spirit-led stance that strengthens boundaries, clarifies decisions, and keeps you from signing the enemy's contracts when you're tired.

When I say holy self-love protects us, even the data nods. Psychologist Kristin Neff has shown for years that self-compassion—treating yourself with kindness, remembering your common humanity, and telling the truth without self-contempt—correlates with lower anxiety and depression and more resilience after failure. A 2012 meta-analysis in *Clinical Psychology Review* reported the same protective pattern across studies, and a 2013 randomized trial by Neff and Christopher Germer found that training people in self-compassion reduced anxiety and stress while increasing well-being. In other words, the posture that helps us repent without collapsing into shame is the same posture that helps our minds

By contrast, simply inflating self-esteem doesn't deliver what the slogans promise. A major review in *Psychological Science in the Public Interest* concluded that boosting self-esteem by itself doesn't reliably improve grades, work performance, or relationships—and can drift into defensiveness when the ego is threatened. Later, work published in *PNAS* found that parental overvaluation tends to cultivate narcissism, not healthy self-worth. Translation: liking yourself loudly isn't the same as loving yourself wisely.

Your body helps tell the truth too. Research in the *Journal of Neuroscience* found that people with better interoception—the ability to sense internal cues like heartbeat—often make clearer decisions under uncertainty. Pair that with the "strength model" of self-control: too many decisions deplete your regulatory energy (decision fatigue), and your yes/no gets wobbly. Practically, that means learning to check in (Holy Spirit + honest body cues) and simplify choices so your boundaries don't crumble when you're exhausted.

Finally, love that's secure loves more cleanly. Classic attachment research and later summaries show that secure attachment—whether you grew up with it or earned it later—predicts healthier boundaries, better conflict repair, and less fear-based people-pleasing. Studies also link self-compassion with more supportive, less controlling behavior in romantic relationships. Spiritually and psychologically, the pattern agrees: the more your identity rests in safe love (for us, in Christ), the less likely you are to sign draining agreements just to keep the peace.

None of this feels glamorous. Most days it looks like a few contested minutes of thought life, a verse spoken out loud in a kitchen, a boundary I keep even when the room doesn't clap. But over time I can feel the difference: fewer hooks for the lie to catch, a clearer channel for the Holy Spirit's witness, a steadier heart that remembers who it belongs to. And that, for me, is what self-love as spiritual protection actually is—staying in agreement with God long enough for the truth to shape the day.

What Is Intuition?

When I say "intuition," I don't mean impulse or mood. I mean that quiet inner knowing—the nudge, the check, the green light—that surfaces when your spirit is listening. Scripture assumes this kind of inner guidance: "My sheep hear my voice" (John 10:27). John even says the anointing "teaches you concerning all things... and is no lie" (1 John 2:27). Intuition, at its best, is your attention cooperating with the Holy Spirit.

When I didn't love myself in Christ, I regularly overrode my own warnings to keep people happy. Holy self-love (agreeing with God about my worth) made it possible to stand up for myself even when no one else was pouring into me. I stopped outsourcing discernment to the loudest voice in the room. I started guarding the wellspring (Proverbs 4:23). And to my surprise, intuition made me stronger.

- **Without self-love:** people-pleasing drowns the inner wisdom; you agree to things your gut and God already said "no" to.
- **With self-love:** you can say a clean "no," not as punishment, but as stewardship of the temple God dwells in (1 Corinthians 6:19–20). That "no" is often your first prophetic act of obedience.

Dr. Lipton has popularized a simple picture: energy can resonate (waves amplify each other) or interfere (waves cancel). Most of us feel this in regular life—some rooms hum with peace; others buzz with agitation. We call it "vibe," "chemistry," or "reading energy." The irony? Humans are the only creatures who routinely train themselves to ignore these instincts.

We are embodied souls, and our nervous systems pick up coherence or chaos. The point isn't to become a vibe-chaser; it's to notice what your body and spirit already know—and then take it to God. Discernment, not impulsivity. Intuition is a *starting signal*; the Holy Spirit is the Interpreter.

Trusting Intuition with the Holy Spirit

Here's how I walk it out so intuition serves the Spirit instead of my ego:

1. **Pause the reflex.** Strong pull or sudden check? I stop. "Holy Spirit, is this You?" If I can't pause, I probably can't discern.
2. **Test by the Word.** God won't contradict Himself. If the "intuition" asks me to violate Scripture or my integrity, it's not Him (2 Timothy 3:16–17).
3. **Check the fruit.** What grows when I follow this nudge—love, joy, peace, patience (Galatians 5:22–23), or panic, pride, secrecy? The Spirit leads; pressure bullies.
4. **Submit it to community.** "Let the prophets speak… and let the others discern" (1 Corinthians 14:29). Wise counsel clarifies signals I might romanticize.
5. **Let peace be the umpire.** If the way forward is God, His peace will keep ruling as I obey (Colossians 3:15). If peace evaporates, I re-check my steps.
6. **Hold timing loosely.** Some impressions are true but **not yet**. "Don't despise prophecies. Test all things, and hold firmly that which is good" (1 Thessalonians 5:19–21).

Prophetic gifts often start with the same sensations we call intuition: a scripture rising unbidden, a sudden compassion for a stranger, a picture in the mind's eye you didn't invent. The difference isn't the channel; it's the

Lordship. New Age "reading" centers *self*; biblical prophecy centers Jesus and His love for others (Revelation 19:10).

To foster this safely:

- **Anchor in Scripture daily.** The more Word in you, the less static in your signal.
- **Practice small obedience.** Share the verse, send the text, pray the simple prayer. Faithfulness expands clarity.
- **Stay humble and coachable.** "We know in part, and we prophesy in part" (1 Corinthians 13:9). Offer impressions, don't announce verdicts.
- **Guard motive.** If I'm using "intuition" to control outcomes or avoid repentance, I've left the Spirit's lane.

Self-love trains a new reflex: I will not betray myself to buy belonging. When a room's energy is flattery up front and contempt underneath, I don't need a spreadsheet to decide—I can feel the interference, and I'm allowed to leave. When the Holy Spirit says, "This door is not yours," I decline, even if it looks like favor. When He says, "This path is yours," I step, even if no one claps.

Practically, I ask three fast questions in hard moments:

- Is this request consistent with who God says I am? (Ephesians 2:10)
- Does saying yes violate a boundary God asked me to keep? (Romans 12:18; Matthew 10:14)
- Do I still have peace as I move toward it? (Colossians 3:15)

Learning to love yourself is about honoring the temple that God chose to dwell in. It's about pouring energy into your soul so that you have something to give to others. As Jesus said, "The good man out of his good treasure brings out good things, and the evil man out of his evil treasure brings out evil things" (Matthew 12:35). If your heart is empty, tired, or broken, what do you have to give? That's why self-love isn't selfish—it's stewardship. If the answers tilt wrong, I don't argue with myself; I honor the temple. That's not pride. That's love.

A simple rhythm to train holy intuition
- **Worship first.** Praise recenters God and clears emotional fog (Psalm 22:3).
- **Name what you sense.** "I feel pressure / I feel peace / I feel anxiety." God works with honesty.
- **Invite the Witness.** "Holy Spirit, bear witness with my spirit" (Romans 8:16).
- **Open the Word.** Ask Him to highlight what is needed today.
- **Act small.** One faithful step beats ten imagined destinies.
- **Review at night.** Where did I sense rightly? Where did I ignore it? Repent, receive, refine.

Intuition isn't a magic trick. It's a muscle that grows as you keep saying yes to the Holy Spirit and no to the lies that once bought your silence. Self-love steadies the hand. Discernment aims it. And over time, the whisper becomes familiar: not because you mastered a technique, but because you learned the sound of your Shepherd and chose to follow.

Living Worthy of God's Design

Learning to love yourself means learning to stop apologizing for being you. It means recognizing when you're shrinking, settling, or silencing your voice—and asking why. It means giving yourself permission to rest, to heal, to say no, to dream again. It means listening to the Holy Spirit when He says, "I will give thanks to you, for I am fearfully and wonderfully made. Your works are wonderful. My soul knows that very well" (Psalm 139:14), and letting that truth shape how you talk to yourself.

Because here's the thing: if you wouldn't speak negative self-talk to a friend, why are you speaking them over yourself? If Jesus paid the highest price for your soul, why treat it like it's disposable?

Loving yourself means walking in agreement with God's love for you. Not in theory, but in practice. It's in how you treat your body, how you speak to your mind, how you protect your spirit. It's in how you set boundaries, how you nourish your soul, how you honor your time. It's not about narcissism. It's about nurturing.

It's also how we learn to love others well. "The second is like this, 'You shall love your neighbor as yourself.' There is no other commandment greater than these" (Mark 12:31). If we don't know how to love ourselves, how can we love anyone else in a way that's rooted in truth and not codependency?

And for me, learning to love myself also meant learning to see that Jesus is for me. When I choose Him, I'm not giving up on my life—I'm choosing the best version of it. I'm choosing joy over fear, wholeness over performance, and intimacy with God over false comfort from the world.

So yes, learning to love yourself is part of the process. Not because you're the center of your story, but because you were made in the image of the One who is. When you care for your life as a sacred vessel, when you steward your gifts with intention, when you speak kindly to the one God is healing—you're loving God, too.

And maybe, just maybe, when you start living like you're already worthy, you'll stop chasing things that were never worthy of you.

Chapter Eleven

Leaving Egypt Because You are Chosen

Cherith is the place God sent Elijah right after he announced a drought to King Ahab. The story sits in 1 Kings 17. After Elijah speaks the word—no rain except at his word (1 Kings 17:1)—God gives him a strange command: "Get away from here, turn eastward, and hide yourself by the brook Cherith, that is before the Jordan" (1 Kings 17:3). There, God promises unusual provision: "You shall drink from the brook. I have commanded the ravens to feed you there" (1 Kings 17:4). And that's exactly what happens—"The ravens brought him bread and meat in the morning, and bread and meat in the evening; and he drank from the brook" (1 Kings 17:6).

But then the water ran out. "After a while, the brook dried up, because there was no rain in the land" (1 Kings 17:7). Elijah hadn't failed. God hadn't changed His mind about him. The assignment had shifted. The word of Yahweh came again: "Arise, go to Zarephath... there I have commanded a widow to sustain you" (1 Kings 17:9). That move leads to the jar of flour and jug of oil that did not run out during the famine (1 Kings 17:14-16), and later to the raising of the widow's son (1 Kings 17:21-22). Cherith is the hinge between public confrontation and private formation, between calling down drought and learning daily dependence.

A few anchors for what Cherith means:

- **Hiddenness by design.** God told Elijah to hide. Cherith is not exile for punishment; it's cover for preparation (1 Kings 17:3).
- **Provision from unlikely sources.** Ravens—ritually unclean birds—become waiters at God's command (1 Kings 17:4, 6). Cherith trains you to receive from places you would never choose.
- **When the brook dries, it's direction, not rejection.** The drying stream wasn't failure; it was the cue to move to Zarephath (1 Kings 17:7–9). Don't worship the method God used yesterday.
- **Cutting and separating.** Many note that *Cherith* ties to a Hebrew root meaning "to cut" or "separate." It fits the season: God cuts Elijah off from old systems so he can be sustained by God's word alone.
- **From power to intimacy.** Before Mount Carmel's fire ever falls (1 Kings 18), Elijah learns the quieter miracles—daily bread, a steady jug, breath returning to a child. Cherith teaches the prophet to trust the Giver more than the gift.

In this book's language, Cherith is a Holy Spirit assignment: a period of purposeful withdrawal where you are fed, trimmed, and re-aimed. It may look like lost momentum—a brook shrinking, doors closing, familiar income streams drying up—but in the Kingdom it's skill-building for the next obedience. Cherith protects you, detoxes your dependence, and proves that your life moves by God's word, not by weather patterns or public approval. When He says "hide," you hide. When He says "go," you go. And between those two commands, you learn the cadence of His voice well enough to follow Him anywhere.

It's also where you learn a quieter lesson: sometimes God hides you so your absence is felt. By the time the brook dried—"because there was no rain in the land" (1 Kings 17:7)—Elijah's disappearance had become a national ache. When God sent him on to Zarephath (1 Kings 17:9) and, later, back toward Ahab, Obadiah testified, "As Yahweh your God lives, there is no nation or kingdom where my lord has not sent to seek you" (1 Kings 18:10). Elijah had been so thoroughly hidden that kings swore oaths trying to prove they'd searched everywhere. In other words, the world missed him.

That is part of the wilderness many of us don't expect. We think hiddenness means we don't matter; in God's economy, hiddenness often reveals that we do. A season of concealment clarifies your weight to others. Your "no" (because God said hide) teaches people not to treat your presence as a commodity. Your absence exposes who only wanted your gift and who truly values your life. It also teaches you—not to chase demand, not to worship doors, not to confuse applause with assignment.

I was 43 the first time I heard of Cherith—the brook where God hid the prophet Elijah during a drought through a sermon given by Pastor Flowers, Jr. of Redefined TV. I was shocked that no one had ever told me before that God hides the things He values most. All my life, I'd been taught to believe that being overlooked, underestimated, or passed over was evidence that something was wrong with me. But what if it was the opposite?

God Hides What Is Sacred

When Heaven wants to protect something precious, it conceals it. That includes you. Sometimes God will isolate you in order to protect and elevate you.

This hidden season is what Scripture refers to as the wilderness. And spiritually speaking, Egypt is everything you once knew—your old habits, mindsets, and patterns. Before you can walk into the Promised Land, you must first be detoxed of Egypt. The wilderness is that in-between place. It's not punishment—it's preparation.

Jesus told parables to help us understand what Heaven is like. And almost every time, He described it as something hidden:

"Again, the Kingdom of Heaven is like treasure hidden in the field, which a man found, and hid. In his joy, he goes and sells all that he has, and buys that field" (Matthew 13:44).

"Again, the Kingdom of Heaven is like a man who is a merchant seeking fine pearls, who having found one pearl of great price, he went and sold all that he had, and bought it" (Matthew 13:45–46).

God hides Heaven not to tease us, but to ensure that only those with sincere hearts and spiritual hunger will find it. You're not just handed glory. You're trained for it.

In the monomyth—the classic hero's journey—the wilderness is the part of the story where the hero leaves the comfort of the known world. It's where they cross the threshold, encounter mentors and tests, and begin their training. Luke Skywalker had Yoda on Dagobah. Frodo had Gandalf, then Sam. Even Jesus had His wilderness—forty days of fasting, temptation, and solitude before His public ministry began (Luke 4:1–2).

Chosen: From Egypt to the Wilderness

"Chosen" doesn't mean favored for comfort; it means set apart for God. Israel heard it first: "You are a holy people to Yahweh your God. Yahweh your God has chosen you to be a people for his own possession" (Deuteronomy 7:6). Not because they were many or impressive—"because Yahweh loves you" (Deuteronomy 7:7–8). And the goal of that choosing wasn't merely escape from pain; it was belonging and assignment: "I bore you on eagles' wings, and brought you to myself... you shall be to me a kingdom of priests and a holy nation" (Exodus 19:4–6).

So when God said, "Let my people go, that they may serve me" (Exodus 8:1), the point wasn't just to get them **out** of Egypt—it was to bring them **to** Himself. That's why deliverance didn't lead straight to Canaan. He led them by a longer, stranger path "lest perhaps the people change their minds" (Exodus 13:17–18). At the Red Sea they learned He could open what looked closed (Exodus 14:21–22). In the desert they learned He could feed what looked empty: "that he might make you know that man does not live by bread only, but man lives by every word that proceeds out of Yahweh's mouth" (Deuteronomy 8:3).

The wilderness was not a mistake; it was formation. "You shall remember all the way which Yahweh your God has led you these forty years in the wilderness, to humble you, to test you, to know what was in your heart" (Deuteronomy 8:2). Egypt had shaped their appetites and reflexes; the wilderness reshaped them around God's presence—a pillar by day, fire by night (Exodus 13:21). Egypt taught survival by fear; the wilderness taught dependence by daily bread. Egypt taught them to belong to a master; the wilderness taught them to belong to God.

Being chosen often includes seasons of hiddenness, like Elijah at Cherith. Not punishment—protection and proof. Your absence starts to be felt; your voice is missed; and inside the quiet you learn the cadence of God's voice well enough to follow Him anywhere. Chosen ones are drawn away so the Holy Spirit can re-tune the heart before re-sending the life.

In Jesus, this call becomes ours: "He chose us in him before the foundation of the world" (Ephesians 1:4). Exiting "Egypt" now looks like renouncing the agreements that enslaved us to fear, shame, and survivalism; passing through the waters looks like baptism—"all were baptized into Moses in the cloud and in the sea" (1 Corinthians 10:2); entering the wilderness looks like learning His voice when provision comes in unfamiliar ways and timing isn't ours to control.

If God has chosen you, expect three movements:
- **Out of Egypt:** out of bondage and false belonging. You're rescued by blood, not hustle (Exodus 12:13).

- **Into the wilderness:** into dependence and re-training. Your diet, desires, and definitions get edited by His Word (Deuteronomy 8:2–3).
- **Toward promise:** not to crown your ego, but to **serve** as a priestly people carrying His presence (Exodus 19:6).

Chosen doesn't make life easier; it makes purpose clearer. It will pull you from predictable slavery into presence-led uncertainty. It will dry up old brooks so you stop worshiping methods. It will confront the Egypt that still lives in your reactions. But it will also give you what Egypt could never give: a name, a covenant, a God who walks with you—day by day—until the land He promised stops being a rumor and starts being home.

Your Personal Exodus

Leaving "Egypt" is not only about getting out of pain; it's about learning who you are when God, not Pharaoh, sets the pace. Israel passed through real water—"the waters were a wall to them on their right hand and on their left" (Exodus 14:21–22)—and then discovered that freedom has its own furnace. The Red Sea was cleansing, but it was not the end. Paul later called that crossing a kind of baptism (1 Corinthians 10:1–2): a new beginning that still requires a new way of living.

This is where the hero's journey gets honest. After the call (Let my people go), there is separation, testing, and the long corridor of formation. The wilderness is the trial phase: hunger that asks, *Who do you trust?* Delays that ask, *Will you wait for God or build a golden calf?* Giants that ask, *Whose report will you believe?* Israel stumbled in each zone, not because the promise was false, but because Egypt still lived in their reflexes.

They carried old appetites into a new season. "We remember the fish... the cucumbers, the melons, the leeks, the onions, and the garlic; but now our soul is dried away; there is nothing at all except this manna to look at" (Numbers 11:5-6). They carried old worship into holy ground. When timing felt unbearable, they fashioned a god they could see and schedule (Exodus 32:1-6). And when God brought them to the edge of promise, they fell into agreement with intimidation. Ten voices said, "We are not able"—"we were in our own sight as grasshoppers" (Numbers 13:31-33). The nation absorbed that report and wanted to go back (Numbers 14:1-4). That's the power of groupthink: ten men talked millions out of what God had sworn.

What they couldn't see in that moment is what Rahab later confessed from inside the land: "I know that Yahweh has given you the land... our hearts melted... for we heard how Yahweh dried up the water of the Red Sea before you" (Joshua 2:9-11). The enemy was already intimidated by what God had done; Israel was intimidated by what they felt. That's a core wilderness trial: will you define reality by fear's report or by God's record?

Part of your personal exodus is accepting that people, places, and habits can't all come with you. Some relationships were Egypt's scaffolding. They made sense in bondage; they collapse under freedom. Some geographies fed old agreements. Some rhythms (cope, numb, perform) cannot survive the diet of daily bread. "Keep your heart with all diligence, for out of it is the wellspring of life" (Proverbs 4:23). To guard the wellspring, you will have to travel lighter. Expect these trials as you move:

- **Provision tests.** Manna trains you to live by God's word, not by panic (Deuteronomy 8:3). When methods dry up, don't worship the old brook; ask for the next word (1 Kings 17:7-9).
- **Worship tests.** When God seems late, your hands will itch for a calf you can control (Exodus 32:1). Wait. He is still the God who fights for you (Exodus 14:14).
- **Identity tests.** Spies will arise—sometimes in your own thoughts—insisting you are a grasshopper. Answer with Joshua and Caleb: "Don't rebel… Yahweh is with us" (Numbers 14:9).
- **Loyalty tests.** Not everyone who walked with you in Egypt can walk with you into promise (Hebrews 12:1). Bless, release, keep moving.

This is why hidden seasons matter. God may hide you so your absence is felt and your dependence is forged, the way He hid Elijah by Cherith (1 Kings 17:3-6; 18:10). Hiddenness is not demotion; it is detox—pulling Egypt out of your instincts so you can carry promise without recreating slavery.

Your exodus will require choices that look like loss in the moment: declining the calf, eating the manna, rejecting the grasshopper story, saying no to old companions who want the comfort of Egypt more than the covenant of Canaan.

But on the other side of those choices is the same reality Israel faced but did not grasp—the world is not unimpressed by what God is doing in you. Hearts are already melting (Joshua 2:11). The only question is whose report you will believe when the wilderness runs hot: the ten, or the One who dries seas and keeps His word.

The Wilderness as Training Ground

If Egypt was extraction and Canaan is assignment, the wilderness is training. Think of it as Ascension Bootcamp: you're on orders, you're learning the terrain, and the Holy Spirit is your commanding Officer. Hiddenness isn't a timeout; it's field school. Bootcamp Rules of Engagement:

- **Signal discipline:** Learn the voice that leads—pillar by day, fire by night. "My sheep hear my voice" (John 10:27).
- **Supply discipline:** Trust today's rations. "I will rain bread from the sky… that I may test them" (Exodus 16:4).
- **Sabbath discipline:** Rest on schedule even when adrenaline says grind (Exodus 16:23-30).
- **Speech discipline:** No grumbling—complaint corrodes morale (Exodus 16:2-3).
- **Squad discipline:** Move as a people; promise is corporate, not solo (Exodus 16:35).

Manna wasn't just food; it was formation. God could have stocked warehouses. Instead He issued a ration that arrived daily, melted in the heat, and spoiled if hoarded (Exodus 16:19-21). The lesson? You don't live by storage; you live by word. "He humbled you... and fed you with manna... that he might make you know that man doesn't live by bread only, but by every word that proceeds out of Yahweh's mouth" (Deuteronomy 8:3).

Bootcamp translation: you're trained out of panic-strategy and into presence-dependence. Yesterday's victory doesn't feed today's obedience; fresh word does. So you report at dawn. You receive what's given. You don't clutch or compare. You eat, you move, you repeat.

Manna was the prototype, not the prize. Israel later kept a jar of it "for generations" as a witness (Exodus 16:32–33), a reminder that God feeds what He calls. Centuries later Jesus made the connection explicit: "It wasn't Moses who gave you the bread out of heaven, but my Father gives you the true bread… I am the bread of life" (John 6:32, 35). Training escalated from flakes on the ground to a Person who nourishes the soul.

And then Jesus handed us a field meal to carry into every wilderness: "He took bread, gave thanks, and broke it... 'This is my body'... 'This is my blood of the covenant'" (Matthew 26:26–28). Communion is not a sentimental snack; it's a covenant ration. In the desert of delayed promise, you don't live on hype; you live on Him. The table says: what manna taught by rhythm, Jesus fulfills by indwelling. Strength for the day, forgiveness for the stumble, presence for the march. Missions You'll Run Out Here:

- **The No-Hoarding Operation:** Gather enough for today. Leave tomorrow to God (Exodus 16:19). Practically: obey the next clear instruction; stop catastrophizing five moves ahead.

- **The Sabbath Test:** Can you stop when God says stop? Boots off, hands open. Rest is warfare (Exodus 16:23).
- **The Water Drill:** When thirst spikes, don't build a calf—ask (Exodus 17:1–6). Provision flows from obedience, not panic.
- **The Intel Operation:** When spies report giants, don't sign fear's contract. Align with Caleb and Joshua: "Yahweh is with us" (Numbers 14:9).
- **The Language Fast:** Replace complaint with worship; God is enthroned on praise (Psalm 22:3).

Bootcamp is intense, but the Holy Spirit also breaks your old seriousness. You learn to laugh at yesterday's "must-have" once manna—quiet, faithful manna—keeps showing up. You learn that ravens can be waiters (1 Kings 17:4–6), widows can be quartermasters (1 Kings 17:9), and a table can be a supply line in the middle of nowhere (Psalm 23:5). The joke is not on you; it's on scarcity because Canaan requires a different metabolism. If you drag Egypt's fear or the wilderness' methods into promise, you'll either crown the calf or hoard the manna. Bootcamp rewires both:

- **From scarcity to sonship:** Daily bread teaches trust so abundance doesn't own you.
- **From noise to knowing:** The quiet tunes your ear so you can move on one word.
- **From grind to grace:** Communion keeps you fueled by mercy, not adrenaline.

So yes—call it Ascension Bootcamp. You're on assignment. You execute the mission in front of you. You eat the ration sent to you. You receive the Body that sustains you. And when the Holy Spirit says "move," you move—lighter, truer, and ready—because the wilderness already taught you the one skill Canaan requires most: how to be led.

Bootcamp has an order of operations: before you carry rank, you learn to take orders. In the Kingdom, authority flows from being led. Israel learned it first—pillar by day, fire by night (Exodus 13:21-22). "You shall remember... how Yahweh your God led you these forty years in the wilderness" (Deuteronomy 8:2). The cadence was simple: He moves, you move. He stops, you stop.

Jesus Himself modeled it: "Jesus, full of the Holy Spirit, returned from the Jordan, and was led by the Spirit in the wilderness" (Luke 4:1). He came out "in the power of the Spirit" (Luke 4:14) and then began to lead others. The path to public guidance ran through private obedience. That's the template.

Moses was led through Midian's obscurity before he led Israel (Exodus 3:1). Joshua served at Moses' side and lingered in the tent of meeting before he carried command (Exodus 24:13; 33:11). David learned to be shepherded—"He leads me beside still waters" (Psalm 23:2)—before he shepherded a nation: "He was their shepherd according to the integrity of his heart, and guided them by the skillfulness of his hands" (Psalm 78:72). Even the centurion understood the principle of authority: "For I also am a man under authority, having under myself soldiers" (Matthew 8:9). Because he lived under authority, his word carried weight. Jesus called that faith "great" (Matthew 8:10).

In Ascension Bootcamp terms, manna, Sabbath, and communion are leadership school:

- **Manna** trains leaders who don't hoard control. You report for daily briefings—"man... lives by every word that proceeds out of Yahweh's mouth" (Deuteronomy 8:3). Leaders who can be fed daily won't starve their people tomorrow.
- **Sabbath** trains pace. If you can't stop when God says stop (Exodus 16:23-30), you'll drive others past grace. Led people lead restfully.
- **Communion** is the command meal that keeps leaders humble: we lead as forgiven ones—"This is my body... this is my blood of the covenant" (Matthew 26:26-28). You don't feed on applause; you feed on Him.

So when you feel hidden, remember: you're not benched—you're being led. Let the pillar set your speed. Let the Word set your diet. Let the Table set your posture. Leaders who have learned to be led carry a different weight: their "Go" doesn't come from grind; it comes from a God they have followed long enough to recognize by voice. "For as many as are led by the Spirit of God, these are children of God" (Romans 8:14). Only then are we safe to lead anyone anywhere.

Walking into a Room with Purpose

Obedience. Healing. Surrender. These aren't just spiritual disciplines—they are the soil in which anointing grows. And anointing isn't about being chosen to be elevated. It's about being prepared to carry something holy. To speak with authority. To walk with peace. To release the presence of God into the world around you without trying to control it.

God doesn't give authority to the loudest voice. He gives it to the most surrendered heart. The quiet ones. The ones who have let Him rebuild them from the inside out. The ones who learned to wait. That kind of authority can't be faked—and it can't be rushed.

There's also a difference between calling and assignment. Your calling is what you were created for—your divine identity and purpose. Your assignment is what God asks you to do in the current season to move in that direction. Assignments can change. Callings don't.

Moses was always called to be a deliverer. But his assignments shifted—from prince to exile to shepherd to leader. David was always called to be king, but his journey took him through pastures, palaces, and caves. Even Jesus, fully God and fully man, spent most of His life unknown, just walking in step with the Father. When the time came for His ministry to begin, He didn't push for it—He stepped into it.

That's the nature of Kingdom purpose: it unfolds in alignment. God is not in a rush. He is in the business of preparation. When you come out of the wilderness, He doesn't launch you into public glory. He entrusts you with a message, a mission, a mantle.

"For we are his workmanship, created in Christ Jesus for good works, which God prepared before that we would walk in them" (Ephesians 2:10).

This is where we stop striving and start stepping. We stop proving and start partnering. We stop asking for signs and start becoming the sign.

The Holy Spirit doesn't give you gifts to define your identity—He gives them to empower your mission. Healing, discernment, wisdom, prophecy, teaching—these are for others. You carry the presence of God not just to feel Him but to release Him. When you've walked through the fire and allowed God to refine you, the fire doesn't consume you anymore—it radiates from you.

That's spiritual authority. That's walking in purpose.

And if you're reading this and wondering if you're ready—I promise, you are more ready than you think.

You've been refined by obedience. You've been reshaped through healing. You've been prepared through surrender. And now you carry something the world needs.

Step forward. Speak the truth. Speak Life. Use your gifts. Tell your story. Share your peace.

Because you were never meant to stay hidden forever.

Chapter Twelve

Refined by the Fire

There are places in life where the terrain grows dark—too dark to see your next step. These are the valleys where the soul is scorched, where faith is no longer theoretical, and where hope feels like a flickering ember in a howling wind. Some call it grief. Others call it trauma. The mystics call it the Dark Night of the Soul.

The dark night of the soul is a sacred, though terrifying, passage. It is not just about grief or hardship—it's a spiritual reckoning. A dismantling. A place where everything you once believed is stripped away, and all the illusions you clung to no longer hold weight. You can't pray the way you used to. Worship feels hollow. Even God's presence can seem distant.

This is what the mystics meant when they described the soul's journey through darkness—not because God is absent, but because His light is so near, it blinds us to everything false. St. John of the Cross called it "a darkening of the faculties," where the soul is prepared for divine union by being emptied of all that is not God.

Facing the Shadows

You begin to face the parts of yourself you didn't even know existed—the bitterness, the pride, the shame, the fear, the control. This is your shadow self—not evil, but unhealed. Not something to fear, but something to bring into the light. We all carry a shadow, and the journey of ascension means being brave enough to look at it, name it, and offer it to God.

But it's not just personal. When we enter the dark night, we are also stepping into what the monomyth calls the collective shadow. In every generation, there is a confrontation with what humanity refuses to see: injustice, greed, spiritual blindness, systems built on fear. And like every hero in the exceptional stories, you will face this shadow not just for yourself, but for others.

In the monomyth—the hero's journey—this part is called the abyss, or the belly of the whale. It's the moment the hero must descend, die to self, and emerge transformed. It is always a death, symbolic or real. A loss of identity, a shattering of ego, and a surrender to something far greater.

But here's the truth the world doesn't often say: you're supposed to feel lost here. You're not broken—you're being broken open. What looks like despair is often the doorway to revelation. You are not being punished; you're being prepared.

I know this valley intimately.

Trauma, Loss, and Spiritual Attack

We had just moved to a new city in 2014—only six months in. I had started a new job, trying to provide a better life for our family. My daughter was in eighth grade, navigating the awkward and often fragile years of early adolescence. I knew she was sensitive, deep-feeling, and thoughtful. I also knew she had been affected when a boy she sat next to in class died by suicide.

I reached out to the school counselor. I began searching for a therapist. I did what I knew to do. But what I didn't know—what I couldn't see—was how close she had come to the edge. I never imagined she would consider doing the same thing. I never believed she could. Two weeks later, I walked into her room to wake her up to go swimming and I found her.

There are no words strong enough to describe the sheer level of fear and horror that came over me. A voice outside of me said: I am in so much trouble. That's when the screaming started and I could feel my mind split. My right brain kept screaming. My left brain assessed the rigor mortis that had already set in, knowing it was too late for me to save her.

It wasn't just grief or even shock—it was evil that seized me. It was a terror so sharp, so otherworldly, that I knew I had come face to face with Satan himself.

For years, I couldn't talk about it. Not the fear. Not the feeling that my daughter had been spiritually attacked. Not the shadow that lingered after. I didn't have the language for what I had experienced, and even if I had, I wouldn't have known who could hold space for it. It took me seven years to admit that I had feared being possessed, to say out loud that I had walked through hell on earth.

The truth is, most parents who lose a child don't make it. And I understand why. The soul gets lost in the shadows, wandering through an invisible wilderness. But even there, somehow—God was with me. Even when I felt like I was being punished for failing my daughter, I was too terrified of the devil to wander too far from God.

Walking Through the Valley of Death

I remember telling my daughter in heaven, "I'm going to show you the way out of the shadow of death." That declaration became my anchor. I couldn't undo what had happened, but I could survive it. And not just survive—but be transformed by it. I knew that if I could walk all the way through this, God would show me how to leave a map behind for others still stuck in the darkness.

Scripture says, "Even though I walk through the valley of the shadow of death, I will fear no evil, for you are with me. Your rod and your staff, they comfort me" (Psalm 23:4). But what it doesn't say is how long the walk might take. Sometimes the valley lasts longer than we think we can endure. But we keep walking, because God does not abandon His children in the dark. He refines them.

"Don't be afraid, for I have redeemed you. I have called you by your name. You are mine. When you pass through the waters, I will be with you; and through the rivers, they will not overflow you. When you walk through the fire, you will not be burned, and flame will not scorch you. For I am Yahweh your God, the Holy One of Israel, your Savior" (Isaiah 43:1–3).

The refining fire doesn't come to destroy us—it comes to reveal what cannot be destroyed. The Holy Spirit didn't yank me out of the shadows. He walked with me in them. And slowly, gently, He began to show me the truth: that this was not the end of my story. That even in unspeakable loss, I could still be made new.

The "shadow self" is what some call the hidden parts of us we'd rather not see—our pain, our rage, our fears, our shame. In Christian terms, this is the part of us that hasn't yet been brought into the light. But we must also recognize that not everything in the shadows comes from within us. Sometimes it's not just our wounds—it's the enemy.

Warfare in the Shadows

Jesus said, "The thief only comes to steal, kill, and destroy. I came that they may have life, and may have it abundantly" (John 10:10). That is spiritual warfare in one verse. The enemy's agenda is destruction. God's agenda is life.

During my valley, I felt the whispers of accusation: *You failed. You weren't enough. It's Your Fault. You Deserve This.* These were not just my thoughts—they were fiery darts (Ephesians 6:16). And I had to learn how to lift the shield of faith against them.

Spiritual warfare is not about shouting at demons—it's about standing firm in Christ. Paul wrote, "Put on the whole armor of God, that you may be able to stand against the wiles of the devil" (Ephesians 6:11). The armor is truth, righteousness, peace, faith, salvation, and the Word of God. When grief opened a door for fear to creep in, I had to speak truth back to the darkness. When accusation came, I had to rest in Christ's righteousness, not my own.

There were nights I woke up paralyzed with terror. Sometimes, I would find myself in Satan's house. Sometimes my daughter had been kidnapped. Other times she held so much contempt for me, she ran away to secretly live with someone else. And yet—even then—I whispered the name of Jesus. Sometimes that was all I could say. But His name has authority. Demons tremble at it (Philippians 2:10).

This is why the dark night is not just psychological—it is also spiritual. The enemy tries to strike hardest when we are weakest. But the same Jesus who descended into the grave also descended into hell itself to proclaim victory (1 Peter 3:19). If He went there and came back holding the keys of death, then He can walk with us in every shadow and bring us through it.

Jesus descended into hell before He rose. And in some ways, so must we. But like Him, we don't go alone—and we don't stay there.

What I've come to understand is that the dark night is not God's punishment—it's His victory. In this season, He is defeating the enemy that has tried to live within us—the sin velcroed to our subconscious, the lies we unknowingly agreed with, the strongholds that kept us bound. It's the process Jesus described when He said, "Let both grow together until the harvest; and in the harvest time I will tell the reapers, 'First gather up the darnel weeds, and bind them in bundles to burn them; but gather the wheat into my barn'" (Matthew 13:30).

The dark night is the separating of weeds from wheat—of truth from deception, of soul from shadow. It feels like tearing, but it is actually cleansing. God strips away illusions, ego, and false security not to torment us, but to rebuild us on rock instead of sand.

St. John of the Cross wrote that the soul is purified through this night until it becomes "so transformed in God that it appears to be God himself and has the same attributes." In other words, the darkness doesn't win—the refining fire of God does.

God's Grace: The Hero's Advantage

In every hero's journey, the tests and trials aren't detours; they are preparation to face the shadow—not only the personal one (old wounds, habits, agreements) but the **collective** one that bends families, systems, and cultures. Scripture names that collective darkness: "our wrestling is not against flesh and blood, but against the principalities... the world's rulers of the darkness of this age" (Ephesians 6:12). How do you stand there without being swallowed? Grace.

As Minister John Bevere argues in his book, *Relentless*, grace is not merely pardon; it is power—God's operational strength at work in weak people so they don't quit mid-story. That squares with the Word: "My grace is sufficient for you, for my power is made perfect in weakness" (2 Corinthians 12:9). Grace doesn't just forgive the soldier; grace fuels the soldier.

When the shadow steps forward, there are only two outcomes in the Kingdom:
1. **Forgive it.** "Don't be overcome by evil, but overcome evil with good" (Romans 12:21). Forgiveness releases

the debt to God's court and severs the hooks of bitterness (Ephesians 4:32). This is how we refuse to mirror darkness back into the world.

2. **Kill it.** Not people—patterns. "Put to death therefore your members which are on the earth" (Colossians 3:5); "those who belong to Christ Jesus have crucified the flesh with its passions and lusts" (Galatians 5:24). In practice this looks like breaking agreements, renouncing lies, and refusing the behaviors that keep the shadow fed.

Grace makes both possible at the same time: soft toward people, ruthless toward sin.

The Holy Spirit is not a distant observer; He is your Advocate in the fight. When fear spikes or doubt hammers, you are not limited to your own supply. Ask to be filled with God's supply:

- When courage fails: "Be strong and courageous... for Yahweh your God is with you" (Joshua 1:9).
- When strength thins: "Be strong in the Lord, and in the strength of his might" (Ephesians 6:10).
- When belief flickers: "I believe. Help my unbelief!" (Mark 9:24).
- When shame returns: "There is therefore now no condemnation to those who are in Christ Jesus" (Romans 8:1).
- When words won't come: "The Spirit also helps our weaknesses... intercedes for us" (Romans 8:26–27).

This is what alignment looks like in the Kingdom: not muscling reality into place, but receiving the grace that aims your will at God's will (Philippians 2:13).

James says to "count it all joy... knowing that the testing of your faith produces endurance" (James 1:2–4). Trials strip away the props Egypt taught us to trust. They unmask the shadow we've been carrying and the shadow in the room we're called to confront. But they also reveal the advantage of sons and daughters: "Let's therefore draw near with boldness to the throne of grace, that we may receive mercy and may find grace for help in time of need" (Hebrews 4:16). At that throne, you don't audition—you receive. How grace moves through the moment:

- **Name it.** Bring the shadow into the light: the lie, the pattern, the resentment. Grace meets truth, not pretenses (1 John 1:9).
- **Choose the weapon.** Is this a forgive-and-release moment (Romans 12:19–21), or a crucify-the-pattern moment (Colossians 3:5)? Often it's both.
- **Ask for God's portion.** "Holy Spirit, fill me with Your courage, Your strength, Your bravery; flood me with Your trust, Your faith, Your belief."
- **Act small and clean.** One obedient step—apology, boundary, blessing an enemy, breaking a habit—lets grace do what striving couldn't.
- **Hold the line with Scripture.** Replace the agreement the shadow offered with the word God has spoken (Matthew 4:4).

The hero's journey in Christ is not the triumph of a rare human; it is the triumph of grace in an ordinary one. You are not alone in the cave. You are not under-resourced at the gate. The same God who pardons your past powers your present, so you can forgive what should have broken you and kill what would have owned you. That is our supernatural advantage: we fight from alignment with God's will, not toward it. And grace—relentless, empowering, unearned—keeps you standing when the collective shadow says you should fall.

Endurance as Victory

So here I am. Ten years later. Still walking. Still being refined. But alive. Restored. Held. Not because I was strong, but because I never let go of my faith. Because I believed in a God who doesn't just dwell in heaven, but enters into our hell to rescue us.

There comes a point in the dark night when the only thing you can do is keep breathing. Keep walking. Keep holding on by the thinnest thread of faith. It feels like nothing is changing, nothing is improving, and you wonder if God has forgotten you. But endurance is its own kind of victory.

Scripture says, "Being confident of this very thing, that he who began a good work in you will complete it until the day of Jesus Christ" (Philippians 1:6). What God starts, He finishes. Even when you feel too weak to move forward, the Spirit keeps carrying the work inside you.

Paul compared the spiritual life to a race, not a sprint, but a marathon: "Don't you know that those who run in a race all run, but one receives the prize? Run like that, that you may win" (1 Corinthians 9:24). Endurance is not glamorous. It is sweat, tears, grit, and the daily decision not to quit. But the crown is promised to those who keep running.

And you are not running alone. Jesus said the Holy Spirit would be our Comforter and Guide: "However when he, the Spirit of truth, has come, he will guide you into all truth" (John 16:13). The Holy Spirit doesn't just whisper encouragement—He empowers you to endure. He steadies your steps when you stumble. He intercedes with groanings too deep for words when you don't know how to pray (Romans 8:26). He testifies within us that we are God's children (Romans 8:16).

Looking back, I realize that endurance was never about my strength at all. It was about leaning into His Grace. There were days I wanted to quit, nights I thought I couldn't take another breath—but somehow, I did. And that "somehow" was the Holy Spirit. He was the One who saw me through.

God's promise is clear: "He who calls you is faithful, who will also do it" (1 Thessalonians 5:24). He will not abandon you in the middle of your story. The same Holy Spirit who led you into this refining fire will also lead you out. And when you emerge, you will not just be surviving—you will be transformed, carrying a testimony of endurance that can light the path for others.

And here's what I know for certain: I know God exists, because I exist. No level of "higher self," no human philosophy, no impersonal source could have carried me through the valley of the shadow of suicide. Only the Holy Spirit of the Living God could walk me through the fire and bring me out the other side resurrected.

The dark night is not forever. It is the threshold between the old world and the new creation. And when the morning comes, when resurrection begins, you will not be the same. You will carry the authority of one who has wrestled with angels, faced their demons, and lived. By the grace of God, I am writing this so you know: there is a way through. You can be made new. Even here. Even now.

Chapter Fourteen

The Land of Milk and Honey

So often in church, we hear stories of people who walked in faith—Noah building a boat when there was no rain, Abraham journeying to a land he'd never seen, Moses parting seas with a staff. These moments can feel like distant miracles, sealed inside a book that's been closed for two thousand years. But Scripture reminds us God's promises are sure—and the path to them forms a people who can carry them.

When Yahweh called Abram, the words were simple and world-shaping: "Go… I will make of you a great nation… you will be a blessing" (Genesis 12:1-3). Promise is never just about possession; it is about becoming. Abundance isn't excess—it is inheritance stewarded in union with the Holy Spirit for the sake of others.

Faith lives in that in-between. Scripture calls it "assurance of things hoped for, proof of things not seen" (Hebrews 11:1). Abraham embodies it: "Who in hope believed against hope… not being weak in faith, he didn't consider his own body… he didn't waver through unbelief, but grew strong through faith, giving glory to God" (Romans 4:18-21). Waiting didn't shrink the promise; waiting trained a heart to hold it. The delays, detours, and deserts do not disprove God—they shape us into the kind of people who won't drop what He places in our hands.

This is where manifesting with the Holy Spirit becomes essential. We are "temples of the Holy Spirit" (1 Corinthians 6:19). When He indwells, He begins to clear the temple—unblocking the flow of life where trauma, bitterness, and hidden agreements with the enemy have clogged the channels (Ephesians 4:27). Unforgiveness—toward others or ourselves—presses like a stone on a riverbed; shame and accusation sandbag the banks. The Holy Spirit lifts those weights through conviction and comfort, while the Word washes us clean (Ephesians 5:26) and the mind is renewed (Romans 12:2).

How do we cooperate? We set our eyes on Jesus (Hebrews 12:2). We enthrone God with praise—"You are holy, you who inhabit the praises of Israel" (Psalm 22:3). We pray in Yeshua's name, we sing when the room feels heavy, and we let Scripture re-author the inner monologue until our thoughts agree with truth. Think of "frequency" here as a shorthand for alignment: as the Holy Spirit clears space in the soul, the heart resonates with heaven's order—peace replaces static, joy displaces dread, love steadies the will (Romans 14:17; Galatians 5:22-23). This is not self-elevation; it is the Spirit raising us into Christ's life (Colossians 3:1-2; Ephesians 2:6).

Call it His ascension in us: the Holy Spirit lifting us out of old loops—trauma, unforgiveness, deceptive agreements—into the mind of Christ. In that alignment, prayer stops feeling like shouting into the wind and starts moving like rivers through cleared channels. The "Promised

Land" becomes more than geography; it becomes a way of being where heaven's inheritance starts to be tasted on earth—"your Kingdom come. Your will be done, as in heaven, so on earth" (Matthew 6:10).

This is the frame for everything that follows in this chapter: promises held through pain, perseverance that becomes identity, and abundance defined as covenant life flowing through a people whose inner temples have been opened by the Holy Spirit to carry what God delights to give.

Sarah & Abraham — Waiting Without Letting Go

God calls Abram out (Genesis 12), seals the promise under the stars—"So shall your offspring be" (Genesis 15:5-6)—and then lets time stretch thin. In the ache of delay, Sarai and Abram reach for a solution: Hagar (Genesis 16). Years later, God sits with Abraham and asks the question that haunts every waiting room: "Is anything too hard for Yahweh?" (Genesis 18:14). At last—"Yahweh visited Sarah as he had said... and Sarah conceived" (Genesis 21:1-2).

Abraham is our pillar of faith—not because he was flawless, but because he kept returning to God. "He didn't waver through unbelief, but grew strong through faith, giving glory to God... being fully assured that what he had promised, he was also able to perform" (Romans 4:20-21). That growth took shaping. He faltered, improvised, protected himself poorly, and still God formed him into a man whose very name was covenant. That's how faith usually looks on earth: not perfect performance, but endurance. Not never failing, but failing better—quicker repentance, cleaner trust, deeper surrender.

The Hagar chapter stands as a loving warning: don't manufacture what only God can give. Ishmael is not a mistake to hate, but a monument to how good ends can be pursued by unbelieving means. The correction isn't shame; it's alignment. When the promise hurts, don't go to Hagar. Go to God.

Adam and Eve mirror the same decision point at a different gate. They chose the serpent's story over God's (Genesis 3:1–6). That's what waiting pressure does: it asks, Whose word will you agree with? Faith is agreement at the gate—before anything changes outside; not a license for control, but a posture of trust in Christ while the Spirit holds you steady.

To "manifest with the Holy Spirit" here means you hold what God spoke without forcing a timeline. You let Him clear your inner temple of fear, hurry, and side deals; you stay in covenant, day after ordinary day. This is how promises ripen without rotting: eyes on Jesus (Hebrews 12:2), hands off the shortcuts, heart anchored in the Word, lips learning to praise in the dark (Psalm 22:3). Practice waiting well by:

- **Gratitude as ballast:** name daily mercies while you wait (Psalm 103:1–5).
- **Honest lament:** tell God the truth about the ache (Psalm 62:8; Psalm 13).
- **Small obedience:** do the next right thing you already know (Genesis 17:1).

- **Guard agreements:** renounce "Hagar" plans; reaffirm covenant promises in prayer and Scripture (2 Corinthians 10:5).
- **Worship on schedule:** sing before you feel it; enthrone Him in the delay (Psalm 22:3).
- **Community check:** let trusted voices reflect God's timing back to you (Proverbs 11:14).
- **Armor up daily:** "Be strong in the Lord... put on the whole armor of God" (Ephesians 6:10–18).
  - **Truth** (belt): counter lies quickly with the Word.
  - **Righteousness** (breastplate): stand in Christ's finished work, not performance.
  - **Peace** (shoes): stay reconciled; refuse offense as a foothold.
  - **Faith** (shield): extinguish fiery darts—fear, urgency, accusation.
  - **Salvation** (helmet): guard your thought-life with who you are in Jesus (Romans 8:1).
  - **Word of God** (sword): speak Scripture out loud; pray it back to God.
  - **Pray in the Spirit**: "with all perseverance" for yourself and others as you wait (Ephesians 6:18).

Theme to carry: Faith doesn't fabricate; it aligns. The God who promised is the God who performs—in His way, in His time. Your part is to keep the gate, choose agreement with His voice, and refuse the detour that flatters urgency but fractures trust.

"Now I Know": When Faith Is Weighed

Abraham's knife raised over Isaac on Moriah is one of Scripture's starkest sentences: "Don't lay your hand on the boy... for now I know that you fear God" (Genesis 22:12). That isn't God discovering new information; it's covenant verification. Abraham's trust is weighed in the scales of obedience and found solid.

Scripture uses this proving language often: God "tests" to reveal what's in the heart (Deuteronomy 8:2), and the "proof of your faith" is "more precious than gold" refined by fire (1 Peter 1:7). James says of this very event that Abraham's "faith worked with his works, and by works faith was perfected" (James 2:22). Hebrews adds the inner calculus: Abraham "accounted that God is able to raise up even from the dead" (Hebrews 11:19). In other words, the scale tips because he trusts God's character.

People sometimes call Abraham's obedience "blind faith," but as John Lennox loves to point out, biblical faith isn't a leap into the dark—it's trust in a trustworthy God. Abraham believed a word from the God who had already proved Himself faithful (Romans 4:20–21). Faith is not credulity; it is reasoned reliance—acting on God's promise *before* the provision appears, because His character is the evidence you carry (Hebrews 11:1). That's why Abraham could climb Moriah. Abraham told Isaac, "God will provide himself the lamb" (Genesis 22:8), and afterward named the place "Yahweh Will Provide" (Genesis 22:14).

Now set that beside Daniel 5. Belshazzar desecrates the holy vessels and exalts himself; the hand writes on the wall:

"Mene, Mene, Tekel, Upharsin." Tekel = "you are weighed in the balances and are found wanting" (Daniel 5:27). Abraham offers back what is most precious and is confirmed. Belshazzar grabs what is holy and is condemned. Same courtroom metaphor, opposite verdicts: one fear of God produces obedience; one contempt for God exposes emptiness.

Revelation extends the weighing to the end of history. "I saw the dead, the great and the small, standing before the throne, and books were opened... and the dead were judged according to their works" (Revelation 20:12). Jesus says, "Behold, I come quickly. My reward is with me, to repay to each man according to his work" (Revelation 22:12). For those in Christ, this is not a fear of losing salvation but a sober accounting of a life's fruit (2 Corinthians 5:10; 1 Corinthians 3:13–15). The question is the same as Moriah: What does your trust weigh when placed on the scale?

Jacob — A Lesson in Holding On

Jacob starts in second place. He comes out gripping his brother's heel (Genesis 25:26). That image sticks because it's his life: backup plans to back up plans. Nothing comes easy. Birthright? Barter. Blessing? Disguise. Wages? Negotiation and spotted sticks. Jacob is the patron saint of "hustling and grinding."

The struggle even moves into his own home, where Leah and Rachel carry the ache we all know—longing to be seen, chosen, secure.

The names of Leah's sons read like pages from a journal:
- **Reuben** — "Yahweh has looked at my affliction; now my husband will love me" (Genesis 29:32).
- **Simeon** — "Because Yahweh has heard that I am hated" (Genesis 29:33).
- **Levi** — "Now my husband will be joined to me" (Genesis 29:34).
- **Judah** — "This time I will praise Yahweh" (Genesis 29:35).

The arc is right there: from *please see me* to *I will praise Him*. Leah's inner war—worth tied to being wanted—begins to loosen. She doesn't get a new husband; she gets a new center. And out of that praise comes Judah, the line of the Messiah, and Levi, the priestly line. God threads redemption through the unloved.

Rachel's ache is different but just as raw: "Give me children, or else I will die" (Genesis 30:1). Envy burns. She offers Bilhah to bear for her (Genesis 30:3-8). Leah answers with Zilpah (Genesis 30:9-13). The house turns into a scoreboard—who's ahead, who's behind—until even intimacy is bartered: mandrakes for a night (Genesis 30:14-16). Leah names Issachar ("wages") and Zebulun ("dwelling")—the vocabulary of transactions (Genesis 30:18-20). At last, "God remembered Rachel... and she bore a son, and said, 'God has taken away my reproach.' She named him Joseph, saying, 'May Yahweh add'" (Genesis 30:22-24). Rachel moves from grasping to gift—from *mine* to *He adds*.

All of it mirrors Jacob's road from grasping to chosen. The conflict in the tent is the conflict in the heart: comparison, bargaining, hustling for love. Leah and Rachel show us what it looks like on the inside when we try to manufacture blessing—how worship turns into wages and people into plans. And then, quietly, how God meets each ache: seen (Reuben), heard (Simeon), joined (Levi), praise (Judah)... until praise becomes the pivot.

Jacob's midnight wrestle at Jabbok echoes this same proving. In the dark, when the last strategy is spent, he clings: "I will not let you go unless you bless me" (Genesis 32:26).

If Moriah asks, *Will you surrender what you treasure?* Jabbok asks, *Will you hold to Me when you have nothing left?* Abraham walks up the mountain on a word. Jacob refuses to release God until the word lands as blessing.

Both scenes expose the heart, and in both, God names the verdict. To Abraham: "now I know." To Jacob: "Israel... for you have striven with God and with men, and have prevailed" (Genesis 32:28).

Jacob moves from heel-grabber to chosen, not by outwitting his brother, but by aligning with God in an encounter that changes his gait and his name. Wrestling with God isn't painless; it often moves from difficult to downright painful.

Jacob limps out of Jabbok (Genesis 32:31), but the truth is the whole house limps—scarred by favoritism, rivalry, and deals. Yet through the limp comes a nation. Through a jealous household comes Judah, through whom the King will come; through Rachel's lifted reproach comes Joseph, who will feed the world in famine. Struggle doesn't get the last word; covenant does.

For us, this is the inner map. When your soul sounds like Leah—*see me, hear me, join me*—or like Rachel—*give me or I die*—that's the place to stop bargaining and start blessing. Manifesting with the Holy Spirit doesn't mean forcing outcomes; it means letting Him clear the temple of comparison and transaction until praise rises again. That's where identity shifts. That's where names change. That's where Israel is born—not out of perfect people, but out of people who finally agree with God in the middle of the mess.

Womb Wounds: When the House Writes the Heart

Ironically—and painfully—what Dr. Lipton argues about early programming rings true in Jacob's tent. Lipton suggests the **subconscious is largely "written" before we can reason**, shaped by the womb and early environment. In Jacob's house, that "environment" was rivalry, comparison, and bargaining—literally **named** into the children: *unloved, hated, wages, dwelling* (Genesis 29:32–35; 30:18–20). If you grow inside a scoreboard, you learn to keep score.

So when Joseph—Rachel's firstborn—arrives, the script is already set. Jacob's favoritism hardens it: "Israel loved Joseph more than all his children… and he made him a coat of many colors. His brothers saw… and they hated him, and couldn't speak peaceably to him" (Genesis 37:3–4). What began as Leah vs. Rachel in the parents' hearts becomes envy vs. favor in the sons' hearts.

Then the old story surfaces—the one as old as Cain and Abel. Cain's jealousy couldn't stand Abel's favor (Genesis 4:3-8). Joseph's brothers say, "Come now therefore, and let's kill him" (Genesis 37:20). Reuben delays the blood (37:21-22), Judah monetizes the envy, and they sell Joseph into slavery (37:26-28). Whether by murder or market, the aim is the same: *remove the favored brother.* What Dr. Lipton would call early "programming," Scripture shows as agreements formed in a charged atmosphere—jealousy, comparison, scarcity.

But God. The Lord writes through crooked lines. What was seeded in the womb and reinforced at the table does not have to be the last word. "You meant evil against me, but God meant it for good, to save many people alive" (Genesis 50:20). Joseph refuses the old agreements—resentment, revenge—and re-signs with heaven: he speaks blessing, establishes boundaries, feeds the very brothers who sold him (Genesis 45:4-11; 50:19-21). The family's "subconscious" script is interrupted by conscious alignment with God.

This is why manifesting with the Holy Spirit matters. If "the life of the flesh is in the blood" (Leviticus 17:11), then the life of the battle is in the mind—where early scripts get replayed or rewritten.

The Spirit enters our temples (1 Corinthians 6:19), exposes inherited lies and learned reflexes, and renews the mind (Romans 12:2). He heals the Cain impulse to eliminate comparison, the Leah ache (*see me, love me*), and the Rachel demand (*give me, or I die*), until praise becomes the pivot again. He trades rivalry for adoption—"you received the

Spirit of adoption, by whom we cry, 'Abba! Father!'" (Romans 8:15).

The womb may have whispered one story, but the Holy Spirit teaches your heart to speak another. In Christ, you aren't fated to replay Leah and Rachel or Cain and Abel. You can become the Joseph or David in your line—the one who breaks the pattern by agreeing with God.

Circling Back to Tomb as Womb

If the house can write the heart, the empty tomb can rewrite it. What began as an inner struggle in Eden—agreement with a lie that fractured the human soul—meets its end in a garden again. On "the first day of the week," Mary Magdalene mistakes the risen Jesus for the gardener (John 20:1, 15). That's not a throwaway detail; it's a synchronicity. Eden is being re-planted. In Adam, the mind agreed with death; in Jesus, life speaks first.

Jesus had already given us the template: "Unless a grain of wheat falls into the earth and dies, it remains by itself alone; but if it dies, it bears much fruit" (John 12:24). A tomb becomes the womb of new creation. He is laid down like seed; He rises with a harvest in view—you and me, made alive with Him.

The curse that wrapped itself around our thinking is addressed at every level. Thorns were the sign of the ground's curse (Genesis 3:18); a crown of thorns is pressed on Jesus' head (John 19:2). The stone that seals death is rolled away (Matthew 28:2). And the Father answers with power: "If the Spirit of him who raised up Jesus from the dead dwells in you, he who raised up Christ Jesus from the dead will also give life to your mortal bodies through his Spirit who dwells in you" (Romans 8:11). The same Holy Spirit who raised Jesus now indwells our temple to end the inner civil war—accusation vs. adoption, shame vs. sonship.

The Reason for Good

The world trained me to hustle and grind. Chapter 8 names it plain: "welfare scum," single-mom ceilings, a recession that made me work for free while paying for daycare, fists clenched on bank-breaks just to survive eighteen months at a job that smiled and sliced. In the middle of that, my stepfather died on a mountain, and our family tore itself raw over addiction. Four years into the climb, I finally landed a career role—then six months later my fourteen-year-old daughter died by suicide. Ten years of PTSD followed. Blame ricocheted—friends, family, me. In 2020 my sister died, my nine-year engagement ended, the two stepsons I'd raised were gone, and I drove across the country half-unstitched, trying to find a self that wasn't built on the sinking sand of trauma.

Chapter 11 names the shadow I carried: a fear that Satan would possess me for seven years, that I had to walk through hell on earth to spare my child her sin and show her how to survive the valley of the shadow of suicide.

In intensive outpatient therapy, someone finally reminded me: But God. "For Christ also suffered for sins once, the righteous for the unrighteous, that he might bring you to God" (1 Peter 3:18). Then four years later, in prayer, I saw a vision of all us sinners across time stepping into Him on the cross. The cross was not a demand for more suffering from me; it was the end of the debt I kept trying to pay from agreements I inherited from my ancestors.

All of this, of course, reaches back to a dream I had at twenty-three while writing a philosophy paper titled "The Reason for Evil." My philosophy professor made a sport of dismantling faith. It was 2004, and he paraded the "God gene" idea from the genome project and the link between temporal lobe epilepsy and mysticism in front of the class, daring us to respond with our amateur concepts. I was one when I had my first seizure from a high fever—and there was no way I was ever going to admit that to him.

Nonetheless, with the final paper lurking, I agreed to tackle the subject. The paper check-ins felt like roast sessions. "Nope, try again," he'd smirk, black frames, black turtleneck, mo-ped helmet sitting on his desk. "You have to provide supporting documentation. Just saying so doesn't make it so, because who are you to have any authority on the subject?"

I kept looking for an argument that would hold. "Nope, try again." The answer, I believed, had finally come in a dream.

In the dream, I was still living at my mother's house. I stood in our one-car garage where my stepfather's tools hung in tidy rows. A serial killer was in the house; I could feel his presence as I rifled through the shadows for a tool to defend myself. His shadow entered the garage. Somehow I slipped past him and ran outside, crouching in the bushes. Breathing hard, I realized I left my body behind, which was still trapped inside. At that point, my only choice was to wait for him to leave.

When he left, I slipped back in, dreading what I would find. The garage had changed into a bigger room, ceiling light on, blood spattered across floor and walls. An orange couch sat where the car should be, its back to me. I took a deep breath as I walked around it. My torso was on the couch—head and legs gone—and my bloody arms cradled a huge ancient book. In gold letters the title read: *The Reason for Good*.

Upon waking up, I knew that this time I had my professor right where I wanted him,

At the next check-in I tried it out: "What about the reason for good?" He didn't blink. "Good is good. No one questions why good exists. Looks like someone has to go back to the drawing board," he taunted.

I finished the paper arguing that human minds can't grasp what it takes for God to address evil born of sin and free will. He signed off on it. But the dream wouldn't let me go. *Why was the Reason for Good the answer to the Reason for Evil?*

Finding Purpose

Some twenty odd years later, I have the answer: the Reason for Evil is the wrong focus. Satan is "the ruler of this world" (John 12:31), the one who said in his heart, "I will ascend... I will make myself like the Most High" (Isaiah 14:13-14). That explains the battlefield.

But why Good? Kingdom and Bible teacher, Bob Mumford, calls it the Agape Road—that God doesn't promise to remove pain but to give it purpose, to form love in the exact places we'd rather close. Mumford calls Jesus the righteous invader—"born of a woman, born under the law" to break the code from the inside and "redeem those who were under the law" (Galatians 4:4–5).

Sin is death; Jesus is life (Romans 6:23; John 14:6). That's the Reason for Good: Life Himself entering a dead system the only lawful way, and showing us how to walk free.

Like Joseph's dreams, mine was a foreshadowing. The serial killer in the house was the Accuser. The tools on the wall were the arguments I kept reaching for. My spirit slipping past him said there was a way out I couldn't engineer. The blood and the missing pieces named the cost. And the book—well, God loves to co-author a good book, doesn't He?

God wrote my story to give my pain purpose. So yes, there is a Reason for Good. He has a name. At a time when evil felt like the only real thing, Life laid His book across my chest and taught me to stand again.

The Universal Christ — An Allegory of Union

Franciscan Father Richard Rohr writes, "God becomes what He loves." This gave me pause—wait a minute, *God loves us.* However, the revelation came when Father Rohr pointed to John's Gospel, where Jesus doesn't only teach—He speaks from union: "I and the Father are one" (John 10:30). John foregrounds that unity and the promise it will be shared with us: "In that day you will know that I am in my Father, and you in me, and I in you" (John 14:20).

If the Synoptics show Jesus as Rabbi moving among us, John lets us hear the I AM speaking from indwelling communion and promising the Helper—so that His life can take shape in ours and we will "do greater works" as He goes to the Father (John 14:12-17).

From there the logic is simple and intimate: our bodies are temples (1 Corinthians 6:19). What happens as we "make room" in the temple? We begin to live our true selves without sin's script—"If anyone is in Christ, he is a new creation" (2 Corinthians 5:17).

Furthermore, John calls Jesus "the firstborn of the dead" (Revelation 1:5; see also Colossians 1:18), and Paul says He is "the firstborn among many brothers" (Romans 8:29). If that is true, then I reasoned the change had to occur with Jesus being baptized in the Holy Spirit.

When I say we "raise our frequency," I'm using a metaphor for sanctification—making room for God's presence through repentance, worship, and the renewing and washing of the mind (Romans 12:2; Ephesians 5:26). Sin creates relational distance—"your iniquities have separated you... your sins have hidden his face" (Isaiah 59:2)—but in Jesus, God reconciled us to Himself (2 Corinthians 5:18-19). The One who seemed far wants to be nearer than our own breath.

And this nearness is not self-ascent; it's gift. The Holy Spirit unites us to Christ so that we live in Him and He in us (John 14:20; 17:21-23). "If anyone doesn't have the Spirit of Christ, he is not his... the Spirit... will also give life to your mortal bodies" (Romans 8:9–11). Jesus is the Firstborn of the resurrection, and we are the children of the resurrection who follow (Luke 20:36).

This, then, is how a person becomes "a new creation" (2 Corinthians 5:17): not by polishing the self, but by consenting to union with God.

Which leads me to ask: Will you allow God love you? To unite with you, work through you, and name who you are in Him? If Jesus shows us what it means to be fully human in God, then manifesting with the Holy Spirit is simply living that union.

I am not saying we become God or equal to God. Scripture is clear: "I am Yahweh, and there is no one else" (Isaiah 45:5). What I mean is that through the blood of the Redeemer we receive access and cleansing (Ephesians 1:7; Hebrews 10:19), and by the Holy Spirit we are united to Christ so His life can actually operate in us—"he who is joined to the Lord is one spirit" (1 Corinthians 6:17). We become "partakers of the divine nature" (2 Peter 1:4) by grace, not by grasping; branches sharing the life of the Vine, never the Vine Himself—"apart from me you can do nothing" (John 15:5). Only in this humble union do we learn what we are truly capable of in Christ: not self-exaltation, but a new creation empowered to will and to work for His good pleasure (2 Corinthians 5:17).

Calling and Assignment: Identity and Mission

Every day now, I ask the Holy Spirit, "What are we doing today?" Because the adventure doesn't stop in the Promised Land. There are still people to reach, truths to uncover, and glory to reveal. And now I walk with God—not as someone trying to earn a place, but as someone who knows she's been sent.

This is what it means to live in spiritual authority: to wake up knowing who you are, whose you are, and what you carry. Not in pride, but in purpose. Not for your own fame, but so the world may know the One who saves.

And as more people are drawn toward spiritual ascension, we—the Church—must be ready to receive them. We must look like Christ. We must carry the fragrance of Heaven. Because if we don't, they'll go elsewhere. They'll be drawn to the nearest thing that feels like light—even if it's false. But it doesn't have to be that way.

You are being refined for such a time as this—not just to be healed, but to become a healer. Not just to ascend, but to help others rise. You are not an observer of God's story—you are living prophecy. You are the walking fulfillment of prayers prayed generations ago.

Manifesting with the Holy Spirit is not about forcing outcomes, bending reality to our will, or chasing after signs. It is about living in alignment with God's presence—so deeply that His Word, His heart, and His Holy Spirit shape the very atmosphere of our lives.

The world teaches us to manifest by self-effort: set your intentions, visualize your future, declare your power. But the Kingdom flips this upside down. True manifestation begins not with self but with surrender. Not with demanding, but with listening. Not with control, but with obedience.

When we align with the Holy Spirit, our lives become vessels through which Heaven flows into Earth. Healing manifests because the Healer lives in us. Provision manifests because the Provider is near. Transformation manifests because the Holy Spirit is always making all things new.

This journey is not linear—it is cyclical, fractal, spiraling like the patterns God wrote into creation itself. Seasons of hiddenness, wilderness, descent, and fire are not setbacks; they are preparation. Every surrender opens space for new life. Every sacrifice becomes an altar where resurrection breaks forth. Every dark night carries the dawn.

And through it all, the Holy Spirit whispers the same invitation: *Walk with Me.* Not tomorrow. Not someday. Now. One step, one prayer, one act of faith at a time.

When you say yes, you are not just manifesting "things"—you are manifesting God's presence in your life. You are becoming the living testimony that His Kingdom is here, that His light shines in the darkness, that His love still heals.

This is what it means to manifest with the Holy Spirit: to let your life become a canvas where God paints His glory. To be transformed from glory to glory. To be made new, again and again, until Christ is fully formed in you.

And so I leave you with this: You were made for this journey. Not to survive, but to rise. Not to control, but to co-create. Not to manifest self, but to manifest Him. The same Holy Spirit who hovered over the waters at creation, the same Holy Spirit who raised Jesus from the grave, now dwells in you.

Step into the secret place. Let the Holy Spirit guide you. And watch as Heaven begins to take shape in the details of your everyday life.

Because this is not the end. This is the beginning. The journey continues. And the Holy Spirit is waiting to walk it with you.

So walk in faith. Speak in faith. Live in expectation.

The King is returning. And He's coming for a radiant bride who knows who she is.

References

Abke, A. (2025). The three beliefs of ego: A sufferer's guide to freedom. New World Library.

Alberino, T. (2020). Birthright: The coming posthuman apocalypse and the usurpation of Adam's dominion on planet Earth. Independently published.

Alberino, T. (n.d.). The Book of Enoch. [Teaching resource].

American Bible Society. (2025, August 14). State of the Bible 2025: Nearly half of U.S. Christians haven't attended church in the past six months. American Bible Society.

Andersen, H. C. (1992). *The complete fairy tales*. Wordsworth Editions. (Original works published 1835–1872)

Arendt, J. (1995). Melatonin and the mammalian pineal gland. Chapman & Hall.

Ascension Presents. (2023, October 22). *Made for worship: Worth-ship | 29th Sunday in Ordinary Time (Fr. Mike's homily)* [Video]. YouTube. https://www.youtube.com/watch?v=[insert-video-id]

Ascension Presents. (2023, November 5). *Made for worship: Kingdom priests | 31st Sunday in Ordinary Time (Fr. Mike's homily)* [Video]. YouTube. https://www.youtube.com/watch?v=[insert-video-id]

Ascension Press. (2017, May 3). Mary: The New Eve and our spiritual mother. Ascension Press.

Barna Group. (2025, April 7). Belief in Jesus rises, fueled by younger adults. Barna.

Baumeister, R. F., Vohs, K. D., & Tice, D. M. (2007). The strength model of self-control. *Current Directions in Psychological Science, 16*(6), 351–355.

Baumeister, R. F., Campbell, J. D., Krueger, J. I., & Vohs, K. D. (2003). Does high self-esteem cause better performance, interpersonal success, happiness, or healthier lifestyles? *Psychological Science in the Public Interest, 4*(1), 1–44.

Bennett, D. (1970). *Catholic charismatic renewal*. Paulist Press.

Bevere, J. (2011). Relentless. WaterBrook Press.

Braden, G. (2001). The lost mode of prayer. Hay House.

Braden, G. (2020). The wisdom codes. Hay House.

Brown, F., Driver, S. R., & Briggs, C. A. (1979). *The Brown–Driver–Briggs Hebrew and English lexicon*. Hendrickson.

Brummelman, E., Thomaes, S., Nelemans, S. A., Orobio de Castro, B., Overbeek, G., & Bushman, B. J. (2015). Origins of narcissism in children. *Proceedings of the National Academy of Sciences, 112*(12), 3659–3662.

Burke, D. L., Field, R. C., Horton-Smith, G., Spencer, J. E., Walz, D., Berridge, S. C., ... Bula, C. (1997). Positron production in multiphoton light-by-light scattering. *Physical Review Letters, 79*(9), 1626–1629. https://doi.org/10.1103/PhysRevLett.79.1626

Campbell, J. (1949). The hero with a thousand faces. Princeton University Press.

Cannon, D. (2001–2015). *The convoluted universe* (Vols. 1–5). Ozark Mountain Publishing.

Catholic Church. (1994). Catechism of the Catholic Church (2nd ed.). Libreria Editrice Vaticana.

Catholic Key. (2024, April 2). Catechism corner | Mary, the New Eve. Catholic Key.

Cook, P. A. (2012). Physics, fractals and flowers. Author.

Centers for Disease Control and Prevention, National Center for Health Statistics. (2025, March 24). *Unmarried childbearing*. U.S. Department of Health and Human Services. https://www.cdc.gov/nchs/fastats/unmarried-childbearing.htm

Centre of Excellence. (n.d.). Spiritual awakening signs. https://www.centreofexcellence.com/spiritual-awakening-signs/

Crean, T. (2022). Mary as a New Eve in the thought of St. Paul. New Blackfriars, 103(1107), 662–677.

Darley, J. M., & Latané, B. (1968). Bystander intervention in emergencies: Diffusion of responsibility. Journal of Personality and Social Psychology, 8(4p1), 377–383.

Dees, G. (n.d.). Gavin Dees [YouTube channel]. YouTube. Retrieved August 28, 2025, from https://www.youtube.com/@GavinDees

Descartes, R. (1989). The passions of the soul (S. Voss, Trans.). Hackett Publishing. (Original work published 1649)

Dispenza, J. (2017). Becoming supernatural: How common people are doing the uncommon. Hay House.

Dispenza, J. (n.d.). Dr. Joe Dispenza official [YouTube channel]. YouTube.

Dunn, B. D., Galton, H. C., Morgan, R., Evans, D., Oliver, C., Meyer, M., ... Dalgleish, T. (2010). Listening to your heart: How interoception shapes decision making. *Journal of Neuroscience, 30*(7), 2707–2715.

Eliot, T. S. (1922/2015). *The waste land.* W. W. Norton & Company. (Original work published 1922)

Eliot, T. S. (1943/2001). *Four quartets.* Harcourt, Inc. (Original work published 1943)

FaithGateway. (n.d.). The Ezer-Kenegdo: Ezer unleashed. FaithGateway. https://www.faithgateway.com

Flowers, J., Jr. (n.d.). Refined TV sermons [YouTube channel]. YouTube.

Furtick, S. (n.d.). Elevation Church sermons [YouTube channel]. YouTube. https://www.youtube.com/@ElevationChurch • Gallup. (2025, June 11). More Americans see religion increasing its influence in U.S. Gallup News.

Gilbert, R. J. (2000). *Sacred geometry and spiritual science* [Lecture series]. Vesica Institute.

Giles, K. (n.d.). Keith Giles blog. Patheos.

Goddard, N. (1941). *Your faith is your fortune.* DeVorss & Company.

Gregorios, P. N. (Ed. & Trans.). (1995). The life of Moses (St. Gregory of Nyssa). Paulist Press.

Guyton, A. C., & Hall, J. E. (2020). Guyton and Hall textbook of medical physiology (14th ed.). Elsevier.

Hawking, S. (2001). The universe in a nutshell. Bantam.

Hawking, S. (2006). The theory of everything. Phoenix Books.

Haney, C., Banks, W. C., & Zimbardo, P. G. (1973). Interpersonal dynamics in a simulated prison.

International Journal of Criminology and Penology, 1(1), 69–97.

Hazan, C., & Shaver, P. (1987). Romantic love conceptualized as an attachment process. *Journal of Personality and Social Psychology, 52*(3), 511–524.

Hernandez, D. (n.d.). David Diga Hernandez [YouTube channel]. YouTube. Retrieved August 24, 2025, from https://www.youtube.com/@DavidDigaHernandez

Hernandez, D. (n.d.). David Hernandez Ministries. Retrieved August 24, 2025, from https://www.davidhernandezministries.com

Heschmeyer, J. (2024, February 22). Why the early Church thought Mary was the New Eve [Audio podcast]. Catholic Answers.

Holy Spirit School. (n.d.). Holy Spirit School: Free Bible-based courses on the Holy Spirit. Retrieved August 24, 2025, from https://www.holyspiritschool.com

Hubble, E. (1929). A relation between distance and radial velocity among extra-galactic nebulae. *Proceedings of the National Academy of Sciences, 15*(3), 168–173. https://doi.org/10.1073/pnas.15.3.168

John of the Cross. (1991). *The collected works of St. John of the Cross* (K. Kavanaugh & O. Rodriguez, Trans., Rev. ed.). ICS Publications.

Joye, S. R. (2025). The metaverse of consciousness: Mapping the multiple dimensions of reality. Inner Traditions.

Jung, C. G. (1969). Archetypes and the collective unconscious. Princeton University Press.

Jung, C. G. (2009). The red book (S. Shamdasani, Ed.). W. W. Norton & Co.

Kavanaugh, K., & Rodriguez, O. (Trans.). (1991). The collected works of St. Teresa of Ávila (Vols. 1–3). ICS Publications.

Kavanaugh, K., & Rodriguez, O. (Trans.). (1991). The collected works of St. John of the Cross (Rev. ed.). ICS Publications.

Klein, D. C. (2007). Arylalkylamine N-acetyltransferase: "The timezyme." Journal of Biological Chemistry, 282(7), 4233–4237. https://doi.org/10.1074/jbc.R600036200

Knowles, M. (n.d.). The face of God: Michael and the Shroud [Video]. YouTube. https://www.youtube.com/watch?v=J8xHAtdFh7Y

Kushner, H. S. (1981). When Bad Things Happen to Good People. Schocken Books.

Lennox, J. (2011). God and Stephen Hawking: Whose design is it anyway? Zondervan.

Lerner, M. J. (1980). *The belief in a just world: A fundamental delusion*. New York, NY: Plenum.

Lewis, C. S. (1944/1996). Myth became fact. In W. Hooper (Ed.), *God in the dock: Essays on theology and ethics* (pp. 63–67). William B. Eerdmans Publishing Company.

Lipton, B. H. (2005). The biology of belief. Mountain of Love/Elite Books.

Lipton, B. H. (2007). *The wisdom of your cells: How your beliefs control your biology* [Audio program]. Sounds True.

Lipton, B. H., & Bhaerman, S. (2009). Spontaneous evolution. Hay House.

MacBeth, A., & Gumley, A. (2012). Exploring compassion: A meta-analysis of the association between self-compassion and psychopathology. *Clinical Psychology Review, 32*(6), 545–552.

MacKenzie, J. A. R. (1978). The patristic witness to the Virgin Mary as the New Eve. Marian Studies, 1640, University of Dayton.

Melmed, S., Polonsky, K. S., Larsen, P. R., & Kronenberg, H. M. (2015). Williams textbook of endocrinology (13th ed.). Elsevier.

Messmer, C. (n.d.). Constance Messmer classes [YouTube channel]. YouTube.

Mikulincer, M., & Shaver, P. R. (2007). *Attachment in adulthood: Structure, dynamics, and change.* New York, NY: Guilford Press.

Milgram, S. (1963). Behavioral study of obedience. The Journal of Abnormal and Social Psychology, 67(4), 371–378. https://doi.org/10.1037/h0040525

Mowczko, M. (2017, December 30). Ezer kenegdo does not mean "a helper subordinate to him." Marg Mowczko. https://margmowczko.com/ezer-kenegdo-subordinate-helper-eve

NASA Earth Observatory. (2003, June 28). *Schumann resonances.* NASA. Observation of Schumann Resonances in the Earth's Ionosphere - NASA Technical Reports Server (NTRS)

NASA Goddard Space Flight Center. (2001). *Ask an astrophysicist: Cosmology Q&A.* https://imagine.gsfc.nasa.gov/ask_astro/cosmology.html

NASA Goddard Space Flight Center. (2024, February 22). *WMAP—Expansion of the Universe.* https://wmap.gsfc.nasa.gov/universe/uni_expansion.html

NASA Science. (2025, March 12). *Solar system: Facts.* https://science.nasa.gov/solar-system/solar-system-facts/

Neff, K. D. (2003). Self-compassion: An alternative conceptualization of a healthy attitude toward oneself. *Self and Identity, 2*(2), 85–101.

Neff, K. D., & Beretvas, S. N. (2013). The role of self-compassion in romantic relationships. *Self and Identity, 12*(1), 78–98.

Neff, K. D., & Germer, C. K. (2013). A pilot study and randomized controlled trial of the Mindful Self-Compassion program. *Journal of Clinical Psychology, 69*(1), 28–44.

Next Level Soul. (n.d.). Next Level Soul [YouTube channel]. YouTube.

Nickelsburg, G. W. E., & VanderKam, J. C. (2012). *1 Enoch: The Hermeneia translation.* Fortress Press. *(See 1 Enoch 7 for the giants "devouring mankind.")*

Ouzounov, D., Pulinets, S., & Freund, F. (2018). Earthquake precursors in atmosphere and ionosphere. *Journal of Asian Earth Sciences, 181*, 103918. https://doi.org/10.1016/j.jseaes.2018.103918

Palvanov, E. (n.d.). Efraim Palvanov [YouTube channel]. YouTube. Retrieved August 22, 2025, from

Palvanov, E. (n.d.). Mayim Achronim [Blog]. Retrieved August 22, 2025, from

Pascual-Leone, A., Nguyet, D., Cohen, L. G., Brasil-Neto, J. P., Cammarota, A., & Hallett, M. (1995). Modulation of muscle responses evoked by transcranial magnetic stimulation during the acquisition of new fine motor skills. *Journal of Neurophysiology, 74*(3), 1037–1045.

Penzias, A. A., & Wilson, R. W. (1965). A measurement of excess antenna temperature at 4080 Mc/s. *The Astrophysical Journal, 142*, 419–421. https://doi.org/10.1086/148307

Pew Research Center. (2025, February 26). Evangelical Protestants now account for 23% of all U.S. adults, and mainline Protestants 11%—both lower than in 2007. Pew Research Center.

Pew Research Center. (2025, February 26). The U.S. religious composition remains stable as Christianity's decline slows. In Religious identity in the United States. [Religious Landscape Study]. Pew Research Center.

Putnam, R. D. (2000). *Bowling alone: The collapse and revival of American community.* Simon & Schuster.

Psychodynamic Awakening. (n.d.). Spiritual awakening symptoms. https://www.psychodynamicawakening.com/spiritual-awakening-symptoms

Quinn, A. (2022). Starseeds What's It All About?: The fast track to mastering ascension. Ozark Mountain Publishing.

Rohr, R. (2016). The divine dance: The Trinity and your transformation. Whitaker House.

Rohr, R. (2019). The universal Christ: How a forgotten reality can change everything we see, hope for, and believe. Convergent Books.

Schmidt, M. (n.d.). Ascension Presents [YouTube channel]. Ascension Press.

Schneider, K. J. (2023, April 3). Passover and the blood of the Lamb [Sermon]. Discovering the Jewish Jesus.

Scott, A. (2010). The pineal gland: Endocrine and spiritual functions. Journal of Alternative and Complementary Medicine, 16(10), 1079–1087. https://doi.org/10.1089/acm.2009.0704

Scribd. (n.d.). Science of Ascension. https://www.scribd.com/document/880189933/Science-of-Ascension

ScriptureCentral. (2024, April 18). How does the Parable of the Ten Virgins offer us direction in life? Know Why.

Sinek, S. (2009). Start with why: How great leaders inspire everyone to take action. Portfolio.

Sinek, S. (2017). Find your why: A practical guide for discovering purpose for you and your team. Portfolio.

StackExchange Hermeneutics. (2014, September 8). In Matthew 25:8–9, what does the oil represent? [Online forum comment].

Steiner, R. (1904). Knowledge of the higher worlds and its attainment. Anthroposophic Press.

Steiner, R. (1910). The way of initiation. Forgotten Books.

Swafford, A. (2025, May 13). Mary: A biblical and patristic perspective. Word on Fire.

Swedenborg, E. (1771/2003). True Christian religion (J. F. Buss, Trans.). Swedenborg Foundation. (Original work published 1771)

Synan, V. (2001). The century of the Holy Spirit: 100 years of Pentecostal and Charismatic renewal. Thomas Nelson.

Szekely, E. B. (1978). *The Gospel of the Essenes*. International Biogenic Society.

Talbot, M. (1991). The holographic universe. HarperCollins.

Taylor, C. (2007). *A secular age*. Belknap Press of Harvard University Press.

Teresa of Ávila. (1980). *The interior castle* (K. Kavanaugh & O. Rodriguez, Trans.). ICS Publications.

The Apocalypse of Moses. (n.d.). In *The Old Testament Pseudepigrapha*. Retrieved from https://www.pseudepigrapha.com

Theology of Work. (2017, February 4). God created woman as an ezer kind of helper (Genesis 2:18). Theology of Work. https://www.theologyofwork.org

TheTorah.com. (2021, October 1). Woman: Helpmate no longer. TheTorah.com.

This Christian Journey. (n.d.). The Ten Virgins, or the qualifications for the kingdom (Matthew). ThisChristianJourney.com.

Thompson, G. J. (2007). An ecological theology of Mary as the New Eve. Collected Essays in Theology.

Underhill, E. (1911). Mysticism: A study in the nature and development of man's spiritual consciousness. E. P. Dutton. Underhill, E. (1914). Practical mysticism. E. P. Dutton.

Udemy. (n.d.). Reiki level 1, 2, 3, and master certification (L. Mohr, Instructor). Udemy.

VanderKam, J. C. (2001). *The Book of Jubilees* (2nd ed.). Wm. B. Eerdmans.

Wolfson, R. (2000). Einstein's relativity and the quantum revolution: Modern physics for non-scientists (2nd ed.). The Great Courses.

Wigglesworth, S. (1999). Smith Wigglesworth on the Holy Spirit. Whitaker House.

Willmington, H. (n.d.). The parables of Jesus Christ: Virgins, vessels, and vigilance. Liberty University Digital Commons.

World English Bible. (n.d.). The Holy Bible: World English Bible (WEB). Public Domain

Wright, E. L. (2017). *Ned Wright's cosmology tutorial.* University of California, Los Angeles. https://www.astro.ucla.edu/~wright/cosmolog.htm

www.ingramcontent.com/pod-product-compliance
Lightning Source LLC
Chambersburg PA
CBHW032104090426
42743CB00007B/234